R. Gupta's®

RPH Scouts and Guides

BE PREPARED!

by

RPH Editorial Board

RAMESH PUBLISHING HOUSE, NEW DELHI

Published by
O.P. Gupta *for* Ramesh Publishing House

Admin. Office
12-H, New Daryaganj Road, Opp. Officer' Mess,
New Delhi-110002 ✆ 23275224, 23245124

E-mail: info@rameshpublishinghouse.com
For Online Shopping: www.rameshpublishinghouse.com

Showroom
- Balaji Market, Nai Sarak, Delhi-6 ✆ 23253720, 23282525
- 4457, Nai Sarak, Delhi-6, ✆ 23918938

Book Code: R-2807

ISBN: 978-93-5477-641-0

Price: ₹ 140

Printed at: Deepak Offset, Delhi

CONTENTS

●●●●●●

SECTIONS OF THE SCOUT AND GUIDE MOVEMENT

SCOUT/GUIDE WING:

Section	Age Group	Name of Unit	Highest Award	Motto
Bunny/Bunny	03-5 yrs	Tamtola	—	Keep Smiling
Cubs/Bulbuls	05-10 yrs	Pack/ Flock	Golden Arrow Award	Do Your Best
Scouts/Guides	10-17 yrs	Troop/ Company	Rashtrapati Scout/Guide Award	Be Prepared!
Rovers/Rangers	17-25 yrs	Crew/ Team	Rashtrapati Rover/Ranger Award	Service

CHAPTER
1

INTRODUCTION

SCOUTING AND GUIDING INTRODUCTION

WHAT IS SCOUTING AND GUIDING?

Scouting and Guiding is a character-building educational movement that supports the growth of young, mischievous youth not only physically but also mentally and spiritually. Scouting and guiding is an outdoor educational movement that aims to help young people develop physical, social, and mental skills to become responsible citizens of the world. Scout Guides are members of this movement who are trained to serve their community, develop their potential, and become better individuals.

"The Bharat Scouts and Guides is a voluntary, non-political, educational movement for young people, open to all without distinction of origin, race, or creed, in accordance with the purpose, principles, and methods conceived by the founder, Lord Baden-Powell, in 1907."

Scouting

Scouting was founded by Lord Robert Baden-Powell in 1907. It initially started as a programme for boys but has since expanded to include all genders in many countries. The main goals of scouting are:

- **Character Development:** Encouraging personal growth and development.
- **Citizenship Training:** Instilling a sense of civic duty and community service.
- **Physical Fitness:** Promoting physical health through outdoor activities and challenges.

- **Skills Development:** Teaching practical skills such as first aid, camping, and leadership.

Scouting activities often include camping, hiking, team sports, and community service projects. Scouts earn merit badges and rank advancements by demonstrating proficiency in various skills and knowledge areas.

Guiding

Guiding was founded by Agnes Baden-Powell and Juliette Gordon Low in 1910, following the establishment of the Boy Scouts. It started as a movement for girls and young women, focusing on their empowerment and development. The main objectives of guiding are similar to those of scouting, with an emphasis on:

- **Leadership Skills:** Encouraging girls to take on leadership roles within their communities.
- **Community Service:** Fostering a sense of responsibility and service to others.
- **Personal Growth:** Supporting emotional, social, and intellectual development.
- **Outdoor Activities:** Promoting an active lifestyle and appreciation for nature.

Guiding activities include camping, crafts, skill-building workshops, and international exchanges. Guides earn badges and awards as they progress through different levels of achievement.

WHY SCOUTING?

The Bharat Scouts and Guides (BSG) emphasises Scouting and Guiding as a means to develop character, discipline, leadership, and a sense of service among young people. The Core Purpose of Scouting and Guiding is:

- **Building Confidence and Self-Esteem:** Scouting helps students build confidence and self-esteem. Through a variety of activities, they develop essential life skills, participate in team-building exercises, and enjoy outdoor adventures and educational experiences. Scouting encourages exploration and discovery beyond the classroom, contributing to the all-round development of young people.

- **Learning by doing:** A core principle of the Bharat Scouts and Guides is 'learning by doing.' Unlike traditional classroom-based education, scouts and guides actively participate in real-world activities. They set up campsites, organise community service projects, and engage in environmental conservation efforts. These hands-on experiences are not just educational but also adventurous, fostering practical skills, problem-solving abilities, teamwork, and adaptability.
- **Community and leadership development:** Scouting goes beyond skill-building to nurture a strong sense of community and leadership. Scouts and guides are encouraged to take on leadership roles within their units and engage actively with their communities. This involvement equips them with valuable life skills, such as effective communication, civic responsibility, and decision-making. It also instills a sense of social responsibility, motivating them to make positive contributions to their communities and the nation.
- **Responsible Citizenship:** One of the fundamental goals of scouting and guiding is to cultivate the concept of responsible citizenship. This goal must be understood in a broad context, emphasising the importance of contributing positively to society and understanding one's role as a responsible citizen.

FUNDAMENTAL PRINCIPLES, AIM, AND VALUES OF SCOUTING AND GUIDING

PRINCIPLES

Scouting/Guiding is based upon three broad principles which represent its fundamental laws and beliefs.

- **Duty to God:** "Adherence to spiritual principles, loyalty to the religion that expresses them, and acceptance of the duties resulting therefrom." This principle recognises that people have different beliefs, and it encourages respect for those beliefs. It reminds Scouts and Guides to honour their own faith and show respect for the faith of others. This duty is about being spiritually aware and respecting the diversity of beliefs in the world.

- **Duty to Others:** "Loyalty to one's country in harmony with local, national, and international peace, understanding, and cooperation." "Participation in the development of society with recognition and respect for the dignity of one's fellowmen and for the integrity of the natural world." This principle is about helping and being kind to others. It encourages Scouts and Guides to be good friends, to lend a hand when needed, and to make a positive difference in their communities. It also emphasises loyalty to one's country and world, friendship, and understanding. It's all about being a caring and responsible member of society.
- **Duty to Self:** "Responsibility for the Development of Oneself". This principle reminds Scouts and Guides to take care of themselves and make the best of their own abilities. It means looking after yourself physically and mentally and striving to improve your own skills and knowledge. This is fully in harmony with the educational purpose of the Scout and Guide movement, whose aim is to assist the young person in the full development of his or her potential–a process that has been called the "unfolding" of the personality.

AIM

The aim of scouting and guiding is fourfold:

1. **Formation of Character**
   - **Building Strong Moral and Ethical Values:** Scouting and guiding emphasise the development of integrity, honesty, and responsibility. These programmes encourage young individuals to make ethical decisions and to act with honesty and fairness in their interactions with others.
2. **Formation of Sound Health Habits**
   - **Encouraging Healthy Lifestyle Practices:** Scouts and guides are taught the importance of maintaining good physical health through regular exercise, proper nutrition, and personal hygiene. Activities such as hiking, camping, and outdoor sports help instill these habits.

3. **Training in Handicraft and Acquisition of Useful Skills**
   - **Developing Practical Abilities and Self-Sufficiency:** Scouting and guiding provide opportunities to learn various practical skills, such as knot-tying, first aid, cooking, and navigation. These skills not only foster self-reliance but also prepare young people to handle real-world challenges effectively.
4. **Cultivation of a Proper Spirit of Service Efficiently**
   - **Fostering a Commitment to Serving Others and the Community:** A core principle of scouting and guiding is service to others. Participants are encouraged to engage in community service projects, helping those in need, and contributing positively to society. This spirit of service promotes empathy, compassion, and a sense of social responsibility.

The pursuit of this aim leads to the development of good citizenship among boys and girls.

VALUES

- **Dharma (Duty and Righteousness):** Scouts and Guides are encouraged to uphold moral and ethical principles, do what is right, and fulfil their responsibilities to society, family, and themselves.
- **Service to Humanity:** Scouts and Guides in India are encouraged to engage in community service, help those in need, and contribute to the well-being of society.
- **National Integration:** Given India's diverse culture, Scouts and Guides learn to respect and appreciate India's cultural diversity and unity, regardless of linguistic differences.
- **Patriotism:** Scouts and guides in India are taught to love and respect their country and take pride in its history, culture, and achievements.
- **Environment Conservation:** Scouts and Guides learn to appreciate and protect the natural world, understanding the importance of preserving the environment for future generations.
- **Leadership and Character Development:** Character development and leadership skills are central to Bharat Scouting and Guiding. Young members are encouraged to develop qualities like honesty, responsibility, and leadership.

MISSION AND VISION OF BSG

MISSION	VISION
"The mission of Scouting is to contribute to the education of young people, through a value system based on the Scout Promise and Law to help build a better world where people are self-fulfilled as individuals and play a constructive role in society."	"The Bharat Scouts and Guides will be a globally visible, consistently growing, self-reliant premium youth movement that is gender balanced, vibrant and responsive to trends. Providing young people with value-based, attractive and challenging youth programme, through competent leaders, effective communication, optimum use of technology and efficient management."

THE FOUR PILLARS OF SCOUTING/GUIDING

PILLAR 1: CHARACTER AND INTELLIGENCE

Scouting and guiding aim to cultivate strong character traits and intellectual growth among participants. Key qualities include:

- **Trustworthiness:** Encouraging scouts and guides to be reliable and truthful in their actions.
- **Loyalty:** Instilling a sense of commitment and allegiance to their country, community, and scouting principles.
- **Courtesy:** Teaching polite and respectful behaviour towards others.
- **Discipline:** Promoting self-control and adherence to rules and responsibilities.
- **Courage:** Developing bravery to face challenges and difficulties.

Character and Intelligence

Character development is fostered through various activities, such as the patrol system, where leadership and teamwork skills are honed. Learning scout laws and lore, engaging in woodcraft, and taking responsibility as patrol leaders are integral to building character. Additionally, activities like team games and camp work encourage resourcefulness and resilience.

PILLAR 2: HEALTH AND STRENGTH

Health & Strength

Ensuring physical fitness and personal health is another cornerstone of scouting and guiding. Participants practice regular exercises like BP's exercises and prioritise good hygiene habits. These activities not only promote physical strength but also contribute positively to their communities.

PILLAR 3: HANDICRAFTS AND SKILLS

Handicrafts and Skills

Scouting and guiding emphasise the acquisition of practical skills and handicrafts. Through activities such as pioneering, bridge-building, and camp expedients, scouts and guides develop problem-solving abilities and leadership qualities. Indoor activities and artistic expression further enhance their skills, fostering creativity and efficiency in their work and daily lives.

PILLAR 4: SERVICE

Service

Service to others and the community is a fundamental aspect of scouting and guiding. Scouts and guides learn teamwork, mutual respect, and understanding of others, which cultivates a spirit of service. This includes practicing religion, performing "good turns" through small actions, and engaging in community service and lifesaving activities. These efforts instil a sense of social responsibility and contribute to the betterment of society.

HISTORY OF THE WORLDWIDE SCOUTING MOVEMENT

THE ORIGIN AND EVOLUTION

The Scouting movement began in 1907 when Robert Baden-Powell, a British Army officer and war hero, organised the first experimental camp on Brownsea Island, off the coast of England. This camp was designed to test his ideas about leadership, self-reliance, and outdoor skills, which he had developed based on his military experiences and observations of youth training. The camp consisted of 20 boys from different social backgrounds who participated in activities such as tracking, camping, woodcraft, and teamwork. The success of this experiment laid the foundation for what would become the worldwide Scouting movement.

Building on the lessons from the Brownsea Island camp, Baden-Powell published Scouting for Boys in 1908, a manual that would serve as the cornerstone of the Scouting movement. Originally intended as a training guide for youth organisations, the book unexpectedly captured the imagination of boys across Britain, leading to the spontaneous formation of Scout patrols and troops. Its focus on adventure, skill-building, and character development appealed to young minds, and soon, Scouting spread beyond Britain to other parts of the world. The movement grew so rapidly that it became necessary to establish a structured framework for organising and supporting local groups.

In 1909, the first major public gathering of Scouts took place at the Crystal Palace Rally in London. This event brought together approximately 11,000 Scouts, showcasing the movement's remarkable growth. However, one of the most significant moments of the rally occurred when a group of girls appeared wearing Boy Scout uniforms,

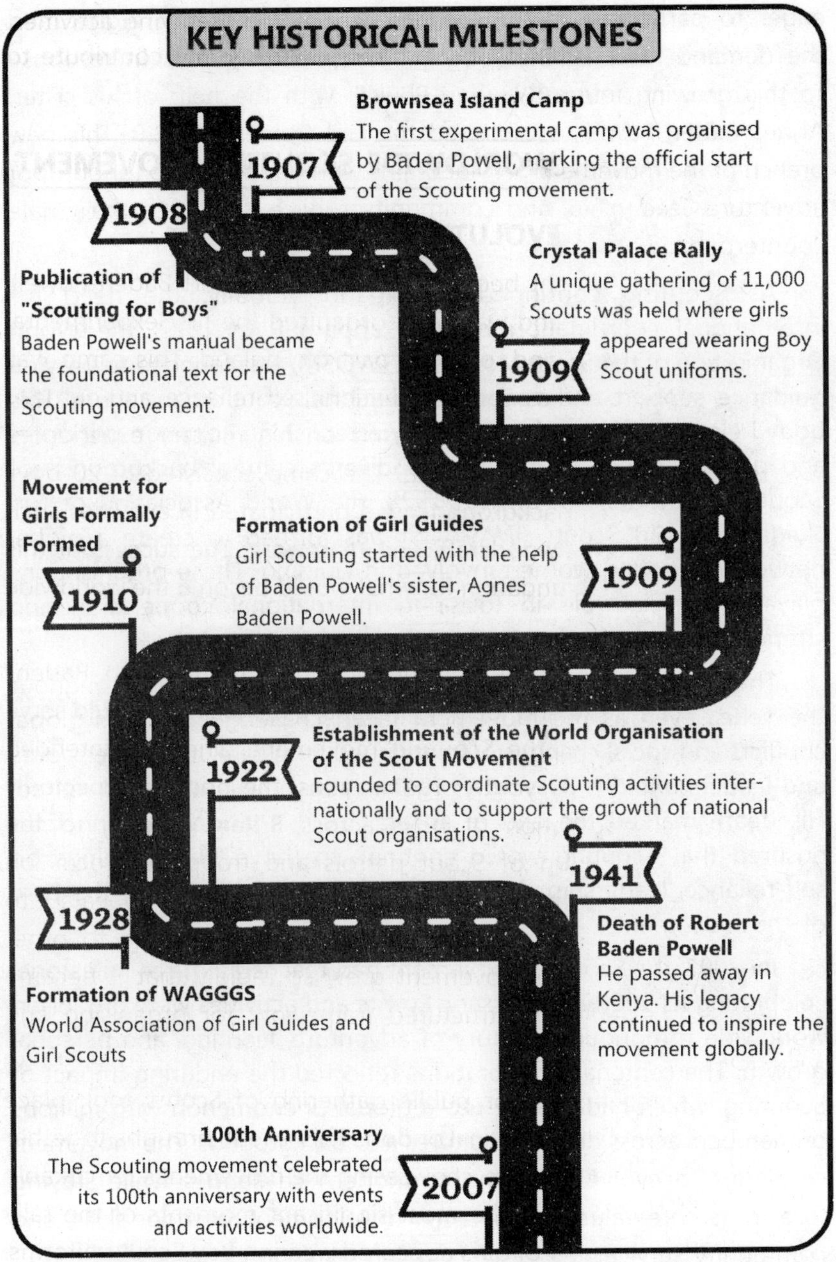
KEY HISTORICAL MILESTONES
1907
Brownsea Island Camp
The first experimental camp was organised by Baden Powell, marking the official start of the Scouting movement.
1908
Publication of "Scouting for Boys"
Baden Powell's manual became the foundational text for the Scouting movement.
1909
Crystal Palace Rally
A unique gathering of 11,000 Scouts was held where girls appeared wearing Boy Scout uniforms.
1909
Formation of Girl Guides
Girl Scouting started with the help of Baden Powell's sister, Agnes Baden Powell.
1910
Movement for Girls Formally Formed
1922
Establishment of the World Organisation of the Scout Movement
Founded to coordinate Scouting activities internationally and to support the growth of national Scout organisations.
1928
Formation of WAGGGS
World Association of Girl Guides and Girl Scouts
1941
Death of Robert Baden Powell
He passed away in Kenya. His legacy continued to inspire the movement globally.
2007
100th Anniversary
The Scouting movement celebrated its 100th anniversary with events and activities worldwide.

eager to participate in the movement. Their presence highlighted the demand for a similar program for young women. In response to this growing interest, Baden-Powell, with the help of his sister, Agnes Baden-Powell, established the Girl Guides in 1910. This new branch of the movement provided girls with opportunities for outdoor adventure, leadership, and community service, similar to their male counterparts.

As Scouting continued to expand globally, the need for international coordination became apparent. In 1922, the World Organisation of the Scout Movement (WOSM) was founded to provide guidance, support, and resources to national Scout organisations. This body helped unify the movement by establishing common principles and practices while respecting the diverse cultural backgrounds of Scouts worldwide. Similarly, in 1928, the World Association of Girl Guides and Girl Scouts (WAGGGS) was formed to create a global network for young women involved in Guiding. These organisations played a crucial role in fostering international cooperation and strengthening the values of Scouting and Guiding.

The influence of Robert Baden-Powell remained strong throughout the years, even as the movement faced challenges such as global conflicts and social changes. He continued to inspire and guide Scouts and leaders until his passing in 1941 in Kenya, where he had retired. His death marked the end of an era, but his vision and principles ensured that Scouting would continue to thrive. His teachings on self-reliance, leadership, and service to others remained at the core of the movement.

By 2007, the Scouting movement had reached a major milestone, celebrating its 100th anniversary. Events and activities were organised worldwide to honour a century of adventure, learning, and personal growth. The centenary celebrations reflected the enduring impact of Scouting, which had grown into a global phenomenon with millions of members across different cultures and backgrounds. The movement continues to evolve, adapting to modern challenges while staying true to its core values of character development, outdoor skills, and community service.

From a simple camp on Brownsea Island to a worldwide movement, Scouting has transformed the lives of countless young people, instilling in them a sense of responsibility, resilience, and a spirit of adventure. Its legacy continues to inspire future generations, carrying forward the vision of Baden-Powell into the 21st century and beyond.

THE SCOUT AND GUIDE PROGRAM IN INDIA

ORIGIN AND EVOLUTION

The Scout and Guide movement in India began in the early 20th century, drawing inspiration from the global Scouting movement initiated by Robert Baden-Powell. British expatriates, who were already familiar with Scouting in the UK, introduced the movement to India, where it quickly took root. The first recorded Scout troop in India was established in Bangalore in 1909 by T.H. Baker, who registered it with the Imperial Headquarters in London. This marked the formal beginning of the movement in India, which soon spread to other regions as Indian youth became increasingly involved.

Between 1910 and 1911, Scout troops were formed in various parts of the country, including Bangalore, Calcutta, Kirkee (Pune), Shimla, Madras, Jabalpur, and Lonavla (Mumbai). These early troops laid the foundation for a structured Scouting framework in India, bringing together young people from different backgrounds and instilling in them the principles of discipline, self-reliance, and service. Recognising the need for similar opportunities for girls, the Girl Guide movement was introduced in India in 1916. The first company of Indian Girl Guides was formed in Pune, following the global trend of involving young women in Scouting activities.

As Scouting gained momentum in India, it became necessary to establish a national organisation to oversee and coordinate its activities. In 1921, the Boy Scouts Association in India was officially formed, providing a structured framework for the movement's

KEY MOMENTS AND DEVELOPMENTS

1909

First Scout Troop in Bangalore
T.H. Baker established first troop in Bangalore and got it registered with Imperial Headquarters London.

1910

Formation of Scout Troops
Scout troops formed in Bangalore, Calcutta (now Kolkata), Kirkee (Pune), Shimla, Madras (now Chennai), Jabalpur, Lonavla (Mumbai).

1916

Girl Guide Movement
First company of Indian girl guides was formed at Pune.

1921

Boys Scout Association in India
Organisation was created to oversee and coordinate scouting activities across country.

1950

Formation of Bharat Scouts and Guides
Boy Scout association and Girl Scout association merged to form Bharat Scouts and Guides.

1951

Official Recognition
Government of India recognised BSG and giving it official status and support.

2005

Digital Integration and Global Participation
BSG began incorporating digital tools and platforms to enhance learning and communication. Also increased its participation in global scouting events and initiatives.

2009

Centenary Celebration
100 years since establishment.

growth and administration. For several decades, the Boy Scouts and Girl Guides associations operated independently, sharing common principles but functioning as separate organisations.

A significant milestone in Indian Scouting history occurred in 1950 when the Boy Scouts Association and the Girl Guides Association merged to form the Bharat Scouts and Guides (BSG). This unification created a single national organisation dedicated to the development of young people through Scouting and Guiding principles. The following year, in 1951, the Government of India officially recognized the Bharat Scouts and Guides, granting it official status and extending support for its activities across the country.

In the 21st century, the Bharat Scouts and Guides continued to evolve, adapting to new technologies and global trends. In 2005, BSG integrated digital tools and online platforms to enhance learning, communication, and engagement among its members. This digital transformation allowed Scouts and Guides to access educational resources more effectively and participate in global Scouting events and initiatives. Through these advancements, the Bharat Scouts and Guides strengthened its presence on the international stage, continuing to uphold the values of Scouting while embracing the opportunities of the modern world.

SIGNIFICANCE OF SCOUTING AND GUIDING IN YOUTH DEVELOPMENT

ROLE IN CHARACTER BUILDING

The movement emphasises the importance of living by a set of moral principles and encourages Scouts and Guides to develop a strong sense of personal ethics. By engaging in community service, teamwork, and outdoor adventures, young people build confidence, resilience, and a positive self-image, all of which contribute to their overall character development.

CONTRIBUTION TO CITIZENSHIP AND COMMUNITY ENGAGEMENT

Community service projects, environmental conservation efforts, and participation in local events help Scouts and Guides understand their role in society and develop a commitment to making a positive impact. This engagement helps them develop empathy, social awareness, and a sense of responsibility towards others.

PROMOTION OF PHYSICAL AND MENTAL WELL-BEING

The movement promotes a healthy lifestyle through various physical activities, such as hiking, camping, and sports. These activities help young people develop physical fitness, coordination, and a love for the outdoors. Additionally, the supportive and inclusive environment of scouting and guiding fosters mental well-being. Participants build strong friendships, develop a sense of belonging, and gain skills to manage stress and challenges.

LEADERSHIP DEVELOPMENT AND LIFE SKILLS

Through various leadership roles and responsibilities, participants learn how to lead, make decisions, solve problems, and work effectively with others. Activities such as organising events, leading patrols, and participating in group projects help them develop critical thinking, communication, and organisational skills.

CHAPTER

2

PRAVESH

SCOUTING BASICS

SCOUT PROMISE

"On my honour, I promise that I will do my best–

- To do my duty to God and my country,
- To help other people at all times,
- To obey the Scout Law."

SCOUT LAW

1. **A scout is trustworthy:** A scout tells the truth. They can be trusted to keep their promises.
2. **A scout is loyal :** A Scout is loyal to their country, scouting, family, and friends.
3. **A scout is friendly and considerate:** A Scout is a friend to all and considers the well-being of others.
4. **A Scout is a brother or sister to every other Scout:** A Scout treats all Scouts as siblings, regardless of differences.
5. **A Scout is courteous:** A Scout is polite and respects others.
6. **A scout is a friend of animals and loves nature:** A scout cares for animals and protects the environment.
7. **A scout is disciplined and helps to protect public property:** A scout is organised and respects community resources.
8. **A scout is courageous:** A scout faces difficulties with bravery and perseverance.
9. **A Scout is thrifty:** A scout uses time, money, and property wisely.
10. **A scout is pure in thought, word, and deed:** A Scout strives for integrity and cleanliness in all aspects of life.

SCOUT MOTTO

The Scout motto is **"BE PREPARED"**. This is achieved by being:

- Physically strong,
- Mentally awake, and
- Morally straight.

SCOUT SIGN

The Scout Sign is made by raising the right hand to shoulder height with the palm facing forward and the thumb holding down the little finger, forming three fingers up.

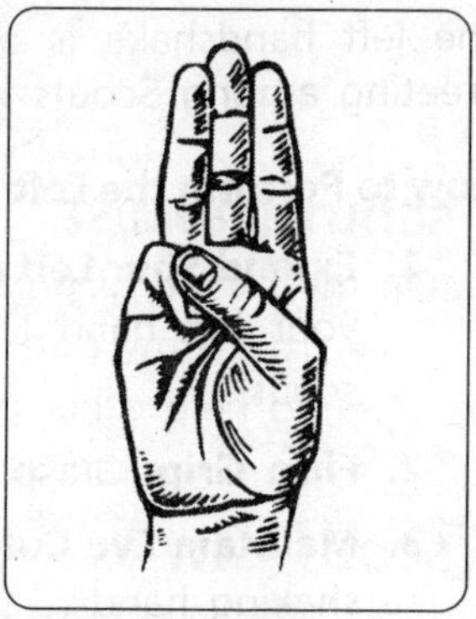

Scout Sign

Meaning of the Scout Sign

- The three raised fingers represent the three parts of the Scout Promise: duty to God, duty to others, and duty to oneself.
- The thumb holding down the little finger symbolises the scout's duty to help and protect the weaker members of society.

SCOUT SALUTE

The Scout Salute is a sign of respect and courtesy, used when greeting other Scouts and during formal ceremonies.

Scout Salute

How to Perform the Scout Salute

1. **Raise the Right Hand:** Lift your right hand to your forehead.
2. **Form the Scout Sign:** The thumb holds down the little finger while the three middle fingers remain straight and together.
3. **Position:** Place the tip of the forefinger just above the right eyebrow or the brim of the hat, if worn.

If a stick or thumb stick is carried, it must be passed to the left hand or kept under the left arm pit.

Meaning of the Scout Salute

- The three fingers symbolise the three parts of the Scout Promise.
- The salute is a mark of respect, showing discipline and unity among Scouts.

LEFT HANDSHAKE

The left handshake is a traditional greeting among Scouts worldwide.

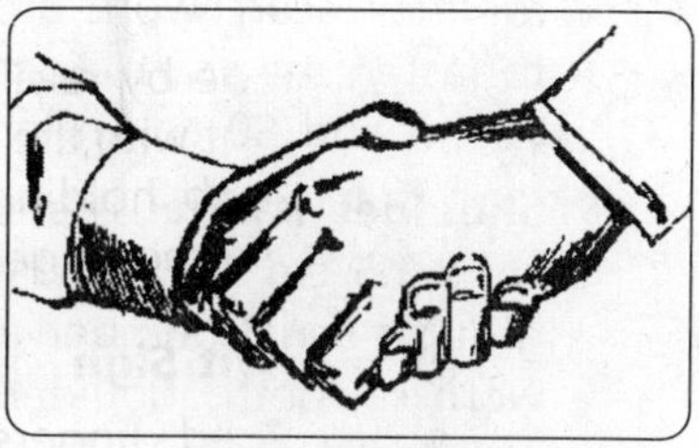

Left Handshake

How to Perform the Left Handshake

1. **Extend Your Left Hand:** Offer your left hand to the other scout.
2. **Firm Grip:** Grasp the other scout's left hand firmly.
3. **Maintain Eye Contact:** Look the other Scout in the eye while shaking hands.

Meaning of the Left Handshake

- **Symbol of Trust:** The left handshake is considered a gesture of trust.
- **Unity and Equality:** The left handshake signifies that all Scouts are equal, regardless of rank or position. It reinforces the bond of friendship and brotherhood within the Scouting community.

SCOUT AND GUIDE UNIFORM

PARTS OF THE SCOUT UNIFORM

- **Shirt:** A steel grey shirt with two patch pockets, shoulder straps, and half or rolled-up sleeves (sleeves may be turned down in cold weather).
- **Shorts or Trousers:** Navy blue shorts or trousers are worn which are comfortable and suitable for active outdoor and indoor activities.

- **Cap:** Dark blue beret cap with the official cap badge. Sikhs may wear a blue turban with the official cap badge. Headwear is compulsory during ceremonies.
- **Belt:** Grey Nylex belt with the official buckle of the Bharat Scouts & Guides.
- **Scarf:** Each troop may have a distinctive colour or pattern for their scarf, worn around the neck with a woggle (a ring to fasten the scarf). Each side of the scarf should be between 70 cm and 80 cm in length.
- **Shoulder Badge:** A shoulder badge should measure 6 to 8 cm x 1.5 cm with a white background, a red border, and the group's serial number and name in red letters. The badge is worn on both shoulders, just below the seam, with a slight curve.
- **Membership Badge:** This is a cloth badge with a green background, featuring a yellow fleur-de-lis superimposed by a trefoil with the Ashoka Chakra in yellow at the center. The badge is worn in the centre of the pleat of the left pocket of the shirt or in the same place on the jersey.
- **World Scout Badge:** This badge is worn in the centre of the pleat of the right pocket of the shirt.
- **Rank Badge:** This is a rank badge designed by the Bharat Scouts & Guides for the specific rank held by the adult leader. It may be worn 4 cm above the left pocket of the shirt or in the same place on the jersey.
- **The BSG Strip:** The name strip containing "The Bharat Scouts & Guides," supplied by the National Headquarters, may be worn just above the right pocket of the shirt.
- **Socks or Stockings:** Black socks or stockings may be worn, with stockings rolled down below the knees and secured with green garter tabs.
- **Footwear:** Black shoes (leather or canvas) with laces are appropriate.
- **Whistle:** A whistle in the Bharat Scout uniform is typically attached to a cord worn around the neck or through a buttonhole for quick access, used for clear communication.

SCOUT UNIFORM

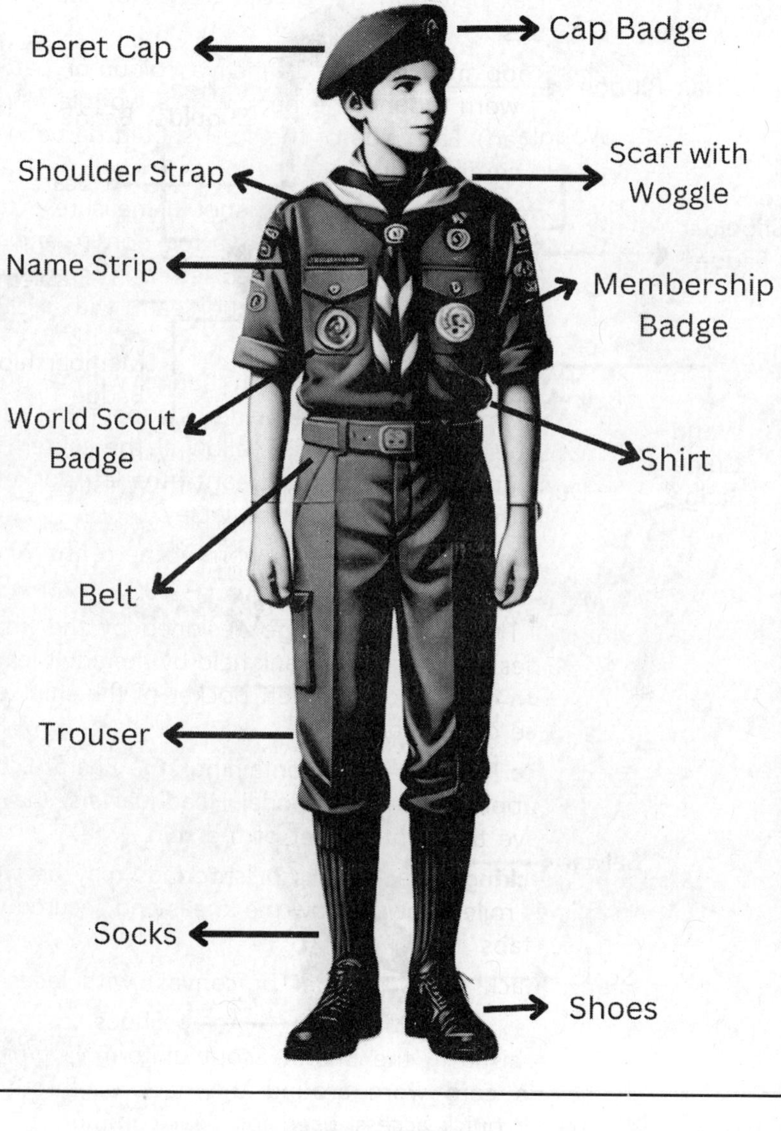

GUIDE UNIFORM

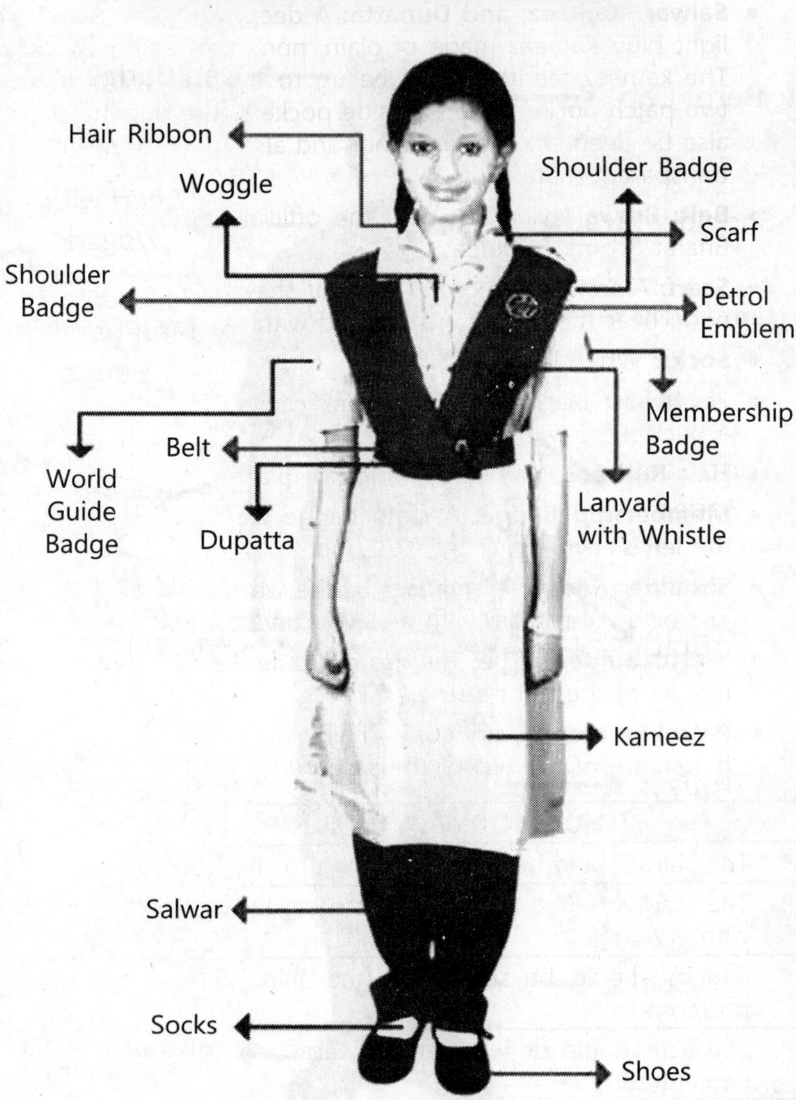

PARTS OF THE GUIDE UNIFORM

- **Salwar, Kameez, and Dupatta:** A deep sky blue Salwar and light blue Kameez made of plain, non- transparent material. The kameez length should be up to the knees and include two patch pockets and two side pockets. The dupatta should also be deep sky blue in colour and also made of plain, non-transparent material.
- **Belt:** Brown Nylex belt with the official brass buckle of the Bharat Scouts & Guides.
- **Scarf:** A scarf in the group's colour shall be worn around the neck, over the collar, and secured with the group woggle.
- **Socks:** White in colour.
- **Footwear:** Black leather or black canvas closed shoes with a buckle.
- **Hair Ribbon:** Plain black ribbon or plain black hair band.
- **Membership Badge:** A cloth badge worn in the middle of the left sleeve.
- **Shoulder Badge:** A shoulder badge worn on both shoulders just below the seam with a slight curve.
- **World Guide Badge:** The World Guide Badge is worn in the middle of the right sleeve.
- **Patrol Emblem:** Every guide shall wear the patrol emblem in the centre of the top of the sash.

HOW TO WEAR THE UNIFORM	
•	The shirt should be neatly tucked into the trousers or skirt.
•	The scarf is folded neatly and worn around the neck, fastened with a woggle.
•	Badges should be sewn onto the shirt in their designated positions.
•	The belt should be worn at the waist, and the buckle should be centred.
•	The cap or hat should be worn straight, not tilted.
•	Footwear should be clean and appropriate for the activities planned.

EMBLEMS AND BADGES

FLEUR-DE-LIS

Fleur-de-lis

The emblem's three petals or leaves represent the Scout Promise's three aspects: duty to God and country, duty to oneself, and duty to others. Lord Robert Baden-Powell, the founder of Scouting, explained that Scouts adopted the fleur-de-lis from the compass rose because it signifies progress in the right direction without deviation. The two small five-point stars symbolise truth and knowledge, corresponding to the ten original Scout laws represented by their ten points. The ring that holds the petals together symbolises the bond of brotherhood within the Scout community.

WORLD SCOUT BADGE

World Scout Badge

The World Scout Emblem is the official symbol of the World Organisation of the Scout Movement (WOSM) and is worn by Scouts and Scouters worldwide to indicate their membership. The reef knot symbolises the strength of World Scouting, while the rope signifies unity among Scouts worldwide. Each national Scout organisation sets specific guidelines for how this emblem should be worn. The World Scout Badge is available in both cloth and metal versions. The cloth badge is typically worn on the uniform, centred on the right pocket pleat, while the metal badge can be worn on various accessories or attire according to the organisation's regulations. Every enrolled member of the scouting movement is entitled to wear the World Scout badge, symbolising their commitment and connection to scouting principles on an international level.

WORLD GUIDE BADGE

World Guide Badge

The World Guide Badge is the official emblem of the World Association of Girl Guides and Girl Scouts (WAGGGS), with its design and colour decided by the World Bureau of WAGGGS. The badge can be made of either cloth or metal and is usually blue with a golden Trefoil at its centre. When worn, the World Guide Badge is placed in the middle of the right sleeve of the uniform. Every enrolled member of the organisation is eligible to wear the World Guide Badge, representing their membership and dedication to the principles of guiding globally.

FLAGS

THE NATIONAL FLAG

The National Flag of India was adopted in its present form during the meeting of the Constituent Assembly held on July 22, 1947, a few days before India's independence from the British on August 15, 1947. The Indian National Flag is a tricolour rectangular panel made up of three rectangular panels of equal width. In India, the term "tricolour" refers to the Indian national flag. The size of the flag is in the ratio of 3:2 (three parts long and two parts wide).

The National Flag of India consists of three horizontal stripes of equal width. From top to bottom, the colours are:

1. **Saffron (Kesariya):** The top band signifies courage, sacrifice, wisdom and action. It also represents the strength and courage of the country.
2. **White (Safed):** The middle band represents truth, peace, and purity. It reflects the light and the path of truth to guide the conduct of individuals and the nation.
3. **Green (Hara):** The bottom band symbolises faith, fertility, and chivalry. It is associated with the prosperity of the land.
4. **Ashoka Chakra:** A navy blue wheel with 24 spokes, known as the Ashoka Chakra, is centrally located on the white stripe. It represents the eternal wheel of law and justice. The 24 spokes signify righteousness, progress, and movement.

Significance

National Flag of India

1. **Unity and Diversity:** The tricolour flag symbolises the unity of India's diverse cultural traditions, languages, religions, and regions.
2. **Freedom Struggle:** The flag embodies the spirit of India's struggle for independence and the sacrifices made by freedom fighters.
3. **National Pride:** It instills a sense of pride, patriotism, and loyalty among Indians towards their country.
4. **International Recognition:** The flag is a symbol of India's identity on the global stage, representing its values and aspirations.
5. **Constitutional Symbol:** As per the Indian Constitution, the National Flag is a solemn symbol of the sovereignty and integrity of India.

The National Flag of India is revered and respected by all Indians, and its hoisting and use are governed by strict guidelines to uphold its dignity and honour.

THE WORLD FEDERATION OF INDEPENDENT SCOUTS (WFIS) FLAG

The flag of the World Federation of Independent Scouts, Germany (WFIS-Germany) is rectangular in shape with a distinctive design, symbolising the organisation. The flag has a 3:2 ratio with a green background. The central feature is the WFIS-Germany emblem, which includes a fleur-de-lis, a traditional scouting symbol, integrated with elements representing Germany. The colours on the flag incorporate the national colours of Germany along with other significant scouting colours, such as green and white. The flag is dark green in colour with a centred light yellow fleur-de-lis that has a red stripe down the centre petal. Below the

WFIS Flag

fleur-de-lis is a light yellow scroll with red letters spelling "WFIS," the organisation's initials, and beneath the scroll is a light yellow square knot symbol.

Significance

1. **Symbol of Identity:** The flag serves as a symbol of identity for WFIS-Germany, distinguishing its members from other scouting organisations.
2. **Cultural Heritage:** By incorporating elements of the German national colours and symbols, the flag also reflects the cultural heritage and pride of the German scouts within the global federation.
3. **Commitment to Scouting Values:** The use of traditional scouting symbols like the fleur-de-lis emphasises the commitment of WFIS-Germany to the core values and principles of the scouting movement, including community service, outdoor skills, and leadership development.

The WFIS-Germany flag is displayed at scouting events, ceremonies, and gatherings to promote unity and pride among members and to showcase their affiliation with the broader World Federation of Independent Scouts.

BHARAT SCOUTS AND GUIDE FLAG

Bharat Scouts and Guide Flag

The Bharat Scouts and Guides Flag is a dark blue flag, with the yellow colour emblem in the centre and Ashoka Chakra in blue. The fleur-de-lis, the international emblem of Scouting, and Ashoka Chakra is meant to emphasise the all-India character of the movement. The superimposed trefoil (three leaves) represents the guide wing of the Bharat Scouts and Guides. The size of the flag is 180 cm. in length and 120 cm. in width, which is a 3:2 ratio. Emblem usually features a combination of traditional scouting symbols such as the fleur-de-lis, often integrated with national elements like the Ashoka Chakra.

Significance

1. **Blue Background:** Blue represents the sky and the limitless opportunities for growth, learning, and exploration available to scouts and guides.
2. **Emblem:** The **fleur-de-lis** is a traditional symbol of scouting worldwide, representing the guiding principles of scouting and guiding, such as duty to God, duty to others, and duty to oneself. The **Ashoka Chakra** represents the eternal wheel of law and righteousness, emphasising moral values and ethical conduct.

WORLD SCOUT FLAG

The flag features a solid purple background, which is a distinctive and symbolic colour for the scouting movement. In the centre of the flag, consists of the World Scout badge in white colour, encircled by a white cord, the ends of which are tied with a reef knot. The size of the flag is in the ratio of 3:2.

World Scout Flag

Significance

1. **Purple Background:** Chosen by the founder of scouting, Lord Baden-Powell, purple is a colour that signifies leadership and service. It is also distinctive and not commonly used in national flags, making it a unique identifier for the global scouting movement.
2. **White Fleur-de-lis:** The fleur-de-lis is a traditional symbol of scouting worldwide. It represents the north point on a compass, guiding scouts on their path to becoming responsible and ethical individuals. It symbolises direction and purpose in life.

   The **three petals** of the fleur-de-lis represent the threefold promises of duty to God, duty to others, and duty to oneself.
3. **Rope and Reef Knot:** Rope signifies the unity and brotherhood of scouts around the world.

Reef Knot symbolises strength and the ability to overcome challenges. It is a knot that holds firmly and does not slip, representing the solidarity and steadfastness of the scouting movement.

4. **Stars:** The stars often symbolise truth and knowledge. They remind scouts to aspire towards higher knowledge and to uphold the truth in all aspects of life.

WORLD GUIDE FLAG

The World Guide Flag was adopted by the 6th World Conference in 1930, following a suggestion from South Africa. The design was created by Frokh Kari Aas of Norway. At the 80th World Community Meeting held in March 1991, a new World Trefoil and World Flag were adopted.

World Guide Flag

The flag features a solid blue background with the Golden World Trefoil in the upper left corner. At the base of the trefoil, there is a flame. The trefoil incorporates two five-pointed stars, one on each side leaf. A blaze of white in the lower right-hand corner represents the peace that Girl Guides and Girl Scouts strive to achieve. This white blaze is crowned by three golden squares, symbolising the threefold promise.

Significance

1. **Blue Background:** Blue represents the sky and the sea, indicating the vastness and international nature of the guiding movement. It also stands for loyalty and trustworthiness, the core values of guiding.
2. **Gold Trefoil:** The trefoil represents the threefold promise made by Girl Guides and Girl Scouts worldwide–duty to God, duty to others, and duty to self. It is a symbol of unity and commitment to the guiding principles.

   Gold Colour: Symbolises the sun, happiness, and warmth, reflecting the positive impact of guiding in the lives of young girls and women.

3. **Flame and vein:** The flame at the base of the trefoil symbolises the flame of the love of humanity and the guiding light that leads Girl Guides and Girl Scouts on their journey.

   The vein pointing upwards represents the compass needle pointing the way.

4. **Stars:** The stars represent truth and knowledge. They remind Girl Guides and Girl Scouts to aspire towards higher knowledge and to uphold the truth in all aspects of life. They also signify the international aspect of the guiding movement, with members spread across the world.

GENERAL GUIDELINES FOR FLAG HOISTING

Honor and Timing

- The flag should be honorably hoisted.
- It should be hoisted after sunrise and lowered after sunset.

Uniform and Arrangement

- Participants must be in complete uniform and arranged in order.
- While hoisting, the flag should be raised completely to the top of the pole.
- Participants should be present when the flag is being lowered.
- All secondary priority officials should stand at the back.
- If a Scout Guide officer or Scout Guides are in plain uniforms, they should stand at the back.

Hoisting and Lowering

- The flag should be hoisted quickly and lowered slowly.
- Salute should not be done while the flag is being lowered.

Special Circumstances

- In case of the demise of any national leader, the flag should be flown at half-mast as a symbol of mourning.

End of the Camp

- At the end of the camp, the flag should be kept on the cleat.
- This should be followed by the national anthem and the announcement of the camp's conclusion.

RULES FOR HOISTING THE NATIONAL FLAG & SCOUTS/GUIDES FLAG

- **Pole Placement:** The pole for the national flag should be 2 feet higher and 2 feet apart from the Scouts/Guides flagpole.
- **Order of Hoisting and Lowering:**
  - The national flag should be hoisted first, followed by the Scouts/Guides flag.
  - In the evening, the Scouts/Guides flag should be lowered first, followed by the national flag.
- **Flag Condition:** A cut or torn flag should not be hoisted.
- **Disposal of Old Flags:** Flags that are no longer in use should be respectfully disposed of by immersing them in flowing water or by burning and burying their remains.
- **Special Circumstances:** In the event of the demise of a national leader or martyr, the national flag may cover the body, but it should be removed before cremation practices are performed.
- **Proper Use:**
  - The flag should not be used for advertising, as window curtains, tablecloths, clothing, or for cleaning tasks.
  - The flag should not touch the ground or come into contact with feet.
  - The flag should be properly folded when it is lowered.
  - The flag should not be inclined in front of anyone except the president of the nation.
  - No other flag should be hoisted to the right of the national flag.
  - No person should stand to the right of the national flag.
- **Handling Scouts/Guides Flag:**
  - Flowers should not be placed on the Scouts/Guides flag.
  - If the flag opens while hoisting, it should be properly adjusted and then tied back.
- **Frequency of Hoisting:** The flag should be hoisted once a day and lowered in the evening.

HOW TO FOLD, HOIST, AND LOWER THE FLAG

Folding the Flag

- **Hold and Fold:** Two people hold the flag at each end. Fold it in half lengthwise, making sure the top toggle and bottom end of the rope are on the same side. This creates a long, narrow shape.
- **Second Fold:** Fold the flag lengthwise again to make it even narrower.
- **Inward Fold:** Fold the flag inward onto itself. If it's a large flag, you might need to do this twice to make it more compact.
- **Roll Up:** Start rolling the flag tightly from the end where it was folded over. This helps to keep it neat and easy to handle.
- **Secure with Rope:** Twist the rope around the rolled flag once. Create a loop at the end of the rope and push it under the twisted part to secure it.
- **Ready for Hoisting:** Now the flag is tightly rolled and secured with the rope, ready to be hoisted up the flagpole.

Hoisting the Flag

- **Flag and Rope:** The flag that is raised has a rope attached to it. At one end of this rope, there's a small wooden block with a knob. This rope is called the "stay." The part of the flag attached to this rope is called the "hoist," and the part flying in the air is called the "fly."
- **Halyard:** The rope used to hoist the flag is called the halyard. It has a knob at the top that fits into the flag block. The other end of the halyard is tied to the flag. This knot is attached to a loop at the end of the rope fixed to the flag using a knot called a sheet bend.
- **Flagpole:** The flagstaff has a rope attached to it, known as the halyard, which slides through a pulley or hole at the top of the staff.
- **Cleat:** About four feet from the bottom of the flagpole, there is a cleat–a small piece of wood or clamp attached to the flagstaff. This is where the loose ends of the halyard are secured.

Hoisting Steps

- Attach the right-hand end of the halyard to the toggle (a small loop or hook) using a clove hitch that slips completely over the toggle.
- Attach the left-hand end of the halyard to the loop at the end of the flag's rope using a sheet bend knot.
- Carefully pull the halyard above the sheet bend until the toggle reaches the top of the pole.
- Hold both ends of the halyard firmly, and wind the pulling rope around the cleat until all the slack is taken up.
- Secure it with a half-hitch knot, making sure not to tug on the halyard that's attached to the flag loop.

Completion: Once secured, the flag is ready to be raised to the top of the flagpole, known as "breaking."

Lowering the Flag

Flag setting is done at sunset or, at the end of the parade, etc. It is not necessary for the entire team to gather under the flag.

- A fully-uniformed member approaches the flagpole.
- Untie the rope, securing the flag.
- Blows a long whistle, signalling everyone to stand at attention facing the flag.
- Slowly lowers the flag with respect.
- Blows a short whistle once the flag is fully lowered, indicating the completion of the process.
- No salutes are performed during this procedure.
- The person who lowers the flag then carefully folds it in an orderly manner, presents it to a superior officer, or stores it appropriately.
- It's important that the scout or guide lowering the flag is in full uniform during this process.

SONGS AND PRAYERS

NATIONAL ANTHEM

जन गण मन अधिनायक जय हे भारत भाग्यविधाता।
पंजाब सिन्ध गुजरात मराठा द्रविड़ उत्कल बंग।
विंध्य हिमाचल यमुना गंगा उच्छल जलधि तरंग।
तव शुभ नामे जागे तव शुभ आशीष मांगे।
गाहे तव जयगाथा।
जन गण मंगलदायक, जय हे भारत भाग्य विधाता।
जय हे, जय हे, जय हे जय जय जय जय हे।।

The national anthem is the pride of India, and Indians are proud of it. Composed by Nobel Laureate Rabindranath Tagore, the anthem highlights India's national heritage and demonstrates patriotism and loyalty to one's country. Adopted as India's anthem in 1950, each verse reflects profound symbolism. Tagore invokes a divine entity, acknowledging it as the leader of all minds and the arbiter of India's destiny. Mentioning regions like Punjab, Sindh, Gujarat, Maratha, Dravida, Utkala, Banga, and geographical features such as Vindhya, Himachal, Yamuna, and Ganga, the anthem celebrates India's diverse cultures and landscapes. It extols the spiritual and physical vastness of the nation, drawing parallels to the Himalayas and the oceans' waves. Ending with prayers for auspicious blessings and the singing of praises, "Jana Gana Mana" embodies India's aspirations for unity, diversity, resilience, and divine guidance, resonating deeply with the nation's ethos and identity.

SCOUT PRAYER

दया कर दान भक्ति का, हमें परमात्मा देना
दया करना हमारी आत्मा में शुद्धता देना
हमारे ध्यान में आओ, प्रभु आंखों में बस जाओ
अंधेरे दिल में आकर के, परम ज्योति जगा देना
बहा दो प्रेम की गंगा, दिलों में प्रेम का सागर
हमें आपस में मिल-जुलकर प्रभु रहना सीखा देना

हमारा कर्म हो सेवा, हमारा धर्म हो सेवा
सदा ईमान हो सेवा व सेवक चर बना देना
वतन के वास्ते जीना, वतन के वास्ते मरणा
वतन पर जान फिदा करना, प्रभु हमको सीखा देना
दया कर दान भक्ति का हमें परमात्मा देना
दया करना हमारी आत्मा में शुद्धता देना।।

The Scout Prayer "Daya Kar Daan Bhakti Ka" was composed by Shri Veer Dev Veer. It is sung in a specific rhythm, standing in solemn silence for 90 seconds. This prayer expresses a deep reverence for God and a plea for compassion, purity, and guidance. It emphasises the importance of serving others and the nation with honesty and devotion. It also seeks divine enlightenment to dispel darkness and unite people in love and harmony.

SCOUT FLAG SONG

भारत स्काउट गाइड झंडा ऊंचा सदा रहेगा,
ऊंचा सदा रहेगा, झंडा ऊंचा सदा रहेगा,
नीला रंग गगन का विस्तृत भ्रातृभाव फैलाता
त्रिदल कमल नित तीन प्रतिज्ञाओं की याद दिलाता
और चक्र कहता है, प्रतिपल आगे कदम बढ़ेगा,
ऊंचा सदा रहेगा, झंडा ऊंचा सदा रहेगा,
भारत स्काउट गाइड झंडा ऊंचा सदा रहेगा,
ऊंचा सदा रहेगा।।

The flag song of the Bharat Scouts and Guides is composed in Hindi by **Mr. Daya Shankar Bhat** of Uttarakhand State. The time it takes to sing the BSG flag song is **45 seconds**.

Scout uses this flag song on different occasions. This verse praises the Bharat Scout Guide flag, emphasising its perpetual height and the symbolism it carries: the expansive blue sky symbolises brotherhood, the fleur-de-lis recalls the three Scout promises, and the wheel signifies continuous progress and advancement. It reaffirms the enduring presence and ideals represented by the flag.

SCOUTING ACTIVITIES

DAILY GOOD TURN AT HOME AND MAINTAINING A DIARY FOR A MONTH

The core principle of scouting emphasises service. While entering the scout movement, scouts and guides take a pledge that they will do at least one good turn every day. It is their duty to fulfil this commitment, and if they forget this one day, they should aim for two acts the next. This work should be done without any selfishness at least once a day and a maximum number of times. This daily good turn should not be anything but small. These acts should be selfless and can be small gestures, starting within their homes. Examples include fetching groceries, assisting with heavy lifting, shining shoes, and helping elders.

After doing a daily good turn every day, scouts have to keep a journal where they record their good turn. This practice promotes self-reflection, personal growth, and the habit of documenting important aspects of their scouting journey.

ATTENDING AT LEAST FOUR TROOP MEETINGS

Scouts are expected to attend a minimum of four troop meetings within a specified period. These meetings are essential for scouts to engage with their troop members, participate in group activities, and learn scouting skills. Troop meetings also provide opportunities for scouts to plan and prepare for scouting events, discuss scouting principles, and receive guidance from troop leaders. Regular attendance ensures that scouts are actively involved in the scouting community and benefit from the structured learning and social interaction within their troop.

Scout aspirants of the unit are required to attend four unit meetings in order to fulfil the Pravesh requirement.

UNDERTAKE A 4 HOUR PURPOSEFUL OUTING WITH HIS PATROL

Scouts undertake a purposeful outing with their patrol, typically lasting for four hours. During this outing, scouts collaborate closely with their patrol members to plan and execute an outdoor activity or exploration. The objective is to foster teamwork, leadership skills, and outdoor competency among scouts. Scouts learn to navigate natural environments responsibly, apply scouting skills in practical scenarios, and develop a deeper appreciation for nature and teamwork. The outing is supervised by trained scout leaders who facilitate learning and ensure safety throughout the experience.

A Pravesh Scout/Guide will work for at least six months to qualify for Pratham Sopan.

CHAPTER 3

PRATHAM SOPAN

PATROL SYSTEM

PATROL

In a Guide Company, the troop is divided into smaller groups called patrols. Each patrol has its own unique identity, including a patrol corner, song, yell, sign, cry, and flag. A patrol typically consists of six to eight members, led by a Patrol Leader. Patrols choose their names based on animals or birds, selected in consultation with the Patrol Council, inspired by Scouting for Boys. Members proudly wear the patrol's shoulder stripes on their uniforms. This structure encourages teamwork and leadership, with the Patrol Leaders and Company Leader collaboratively managing the Guide Company.

COMPANY

The company comprises 24-32 guides, which includes the company leader, assistant company leader, patrol leader, and their seconds. This company is divided into four patrols, with each patrol consisting of 6-8 members. The overall leadership of the company is entrusted to the company leader, who operates under the supervision and guidance of the unit leader.

TROOP LEADER

A Patrol Leader, with at least six months of service and preferably holding the Dwitiya Sopan Badge, is appointed as the Troop Leader by the Scout Master in consultation with the Court of Honour. The troop leader wears the Scout uniform, distinguished by three green

Troop Leader Badge

vertical stripes (6 cm long and 1.5 cm wide) on the left pocket. These stripes are made of wool or cotton, with the middle stripe placed under the membership badge and the other two on either side. He also wears the troop leader's badge. It is a rectangular emblem with a yellow design on a green background and a yellow ring around it. It is worn above the service star on the left pocket or jersey. This leader provides active assistance to the Scout Master and Assistant Scout Master and assumes leadership in their absence.

Troop Leader Pocket

ASSISTANT TROOP LEADER

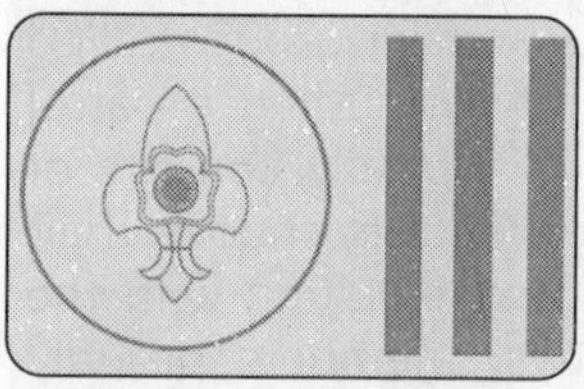
Assistant Troop Leader

An experienced Patrol Leader, preferably with the Dwitiya Sopan Badge, is appointed as Assistant Troop Leader by the Scout Master in consultation with the Court of Honour. The Assistant Troop Leader wears the Scout uniform with two green stripes on the left pocket and the Assistant Troop Leader's badge above the left pocket or on the uniform. The Assistant Troop Leader's Badge is rectangular, featuring an emblem and ring in green, with three green vertical stripes to the left of the emblem. They assist the troop leader as directed.

Assistant Pocket

COMPANY LEADER (FOR GUIDES)

Similarly, a patrol leader with at least six months of service and the Dwitiya Sopan badge is appointed as company leader by the guide captain in consultation with the Court of Honour. The Company Leader wears the Guide Uniform with three green armlets stitched over the cuff of the left sleeve, spaced 1 cm apart, and the Company Leader Badge with its base 4 cm above the right sleeve. The Company Leader's Badge is rectangular, featuring a yellow emblem on a green background with a yellow ring and three vertical green stripes to the left of the emblem. They assist the guide captain and assistant guide captain, taking charge of the unit in their absence.

ASSISTANT COMPANY LEADER (FOR GUIDES)

Similarly, a Patrol Leader with the Dwitiya Sopan Badge is appointed as Assistant Company Leader by the Guide Captain in consultation with the Court of Honour. The Assistant Company Leader wears the Guide Uniform with three green armlets stitched over the cuff of the left sleeve, spaced 1 cm apart, and the Assistant Company Leader's Badge with its base 4 cm above the right sleeve. Their badge is rectangular, with an emblem and ring in green and three green vertical stripes to the left of the emblem. They assist the company leader as directed.

PATROL LEADER

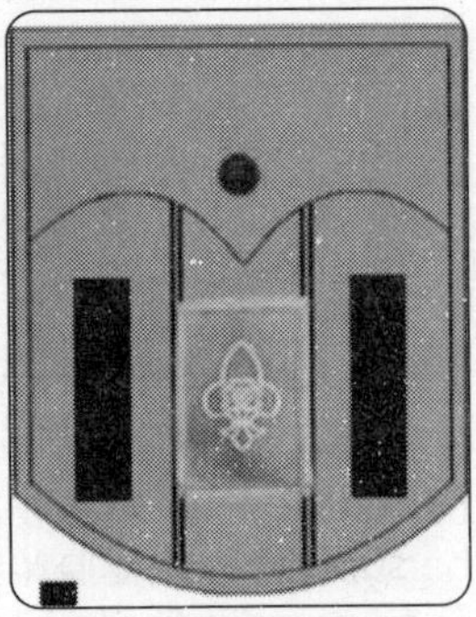

Patrol Leader Pocket

Each patrol is led by a Patrol Leader appointed by the Scout Master in consultation with the Court of Honour and the patrol members. The patrol leader wears the Scout uniform with two green stripes on either side of the membership badge on the left pocket and carries the patrol flag. Similarly, in guides, a patrol leader is appointed by the guide captain in consultation with the court of honour, and patrol members lead each patrol. The Guide Patrol Leader wears the Guide uniform with two green armlets stitched over the cuff of the left sleeve, spaced 1 cm apart.

ASSISTANT PATROL LEADER (SECOND)

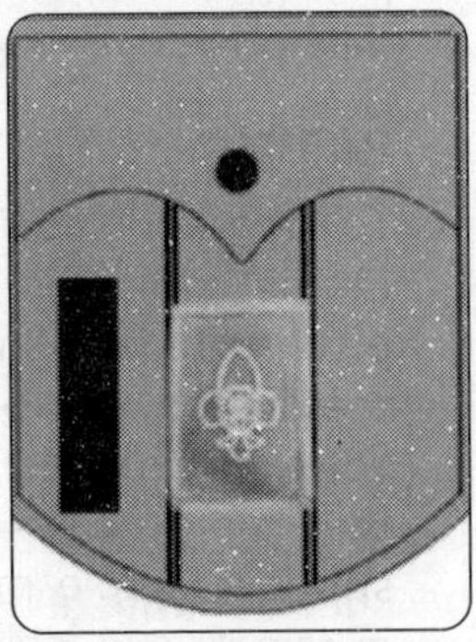

Assistant Patrol Leader Pocket

Each patrol also has a second, selected by the patrol leader with approval from the scout master and the court of honour. The second assists the patrol leader and assumes their responsibilities in their absence. They wear the Scout uniform with one green stripe on the right side of the membership badge on the left pocket. In guides, the second, selected by the patrol leader with approval from the guide captain and the court of honour, helps the patrol leader and fills in for them when needed. They wear the Guide Uniform with one green armlet, 1.5 cm wide, stitched over the cuff of the left sleeve, positioned 1 cm above the lower edge.

PATROL IDENTITY

PATROL NAMES

Patrols can select engaging names that reflect the interests and local influences of the scouts and guides. Each patrol should have a distinctive name that captures its unique identity and spirit. Typically, patrols are named after flowers, a choice made in consultation with the patrol council.

EMBLEMS

The patrol emblem is circular, with a diameter of 5 cm. It features a black background surrounded by a green border. In the centre of the circle, the emblem depicts the flower in its original colour. For example, a rose would be pink, sunflowers yellow, a lotus red, a jasmine white etc.

Patrol Emblems

Members of each patrol shall proudly wear the emblem of their respective patrol on their uniform, above the left pocket, or at the same place on the sash. The emblem serves as a distinctive symbol for the patrol, used on the patrol flag, medallions on Scout shirts, in the patrol den, on patrol equipment, and as a unique signature for the patrol.

PATROL FLAG

To create a patrol flag, scouts must divide their group into buddy teams and challenge each team to produce a rough sketch. Then display these sketches for everyone to see and vote on the best design. Once chosen, they can proceed to make the flag using strong, durable material that won't fade in rain or sun; colours like green or light khaki are recommended.

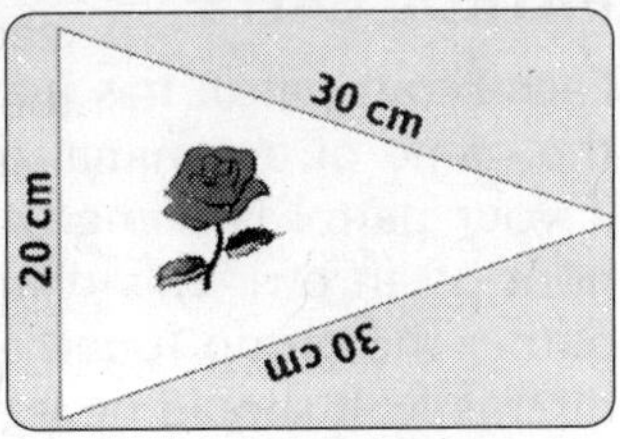

Patrol Flag

Making the patrol flag should be a collaborative effort. Tasks can be assigned accordingly: one boy for the final design, another to procure the material and transfer the design, and yet another for painting. Tasks like cutting and carving the staff and arranging streamers for the top can involve different boys too.

The patrol flag should be triangular, white in colour, with the patrol emblem in red. The base should measure 20 cm, with each side measuring 30 cm. The flag is typically carried by the patrol leader. Each patrol's flag proudly displays its unique emblem. One thing to Remember is best flags are those designed and made by the patrol itself. Regardless of the original colour of the flower emblem, it should always appear in red on the patrol flag.

PATROL YELL

A patrol yell is a cheer that boosts morale and demonstrates team spirit. It's used by Scouts to celebrate victories or announce accomplishments. Scouts gather their patrol close together and shout loudly and enthusiastically. This helps unify the patrol and shows pride in their achievements.

PATROL SONG

Creating a patrol song is an excellent way to boost patrol spirit and unity. Start by working together with the patrol to craft a short song that captures the group's activities and values. Explore different melodies that everyone enjoys singing. Once you find a suitable tune, focus on writing lyrics that hold special meaning for the patrol. If needed, seek assistance from a teacher, a local writer, or someone experienced in songwriting. Once the song is finished, teach it to the patrol and use it on various occasions to reinforce the group's identity and spirit.

PATROL CALLS

Each scout patrol has its own unique patrol call, typically reflecting the name of an animal or bird chosen by the patrol. For example, if your patrol is named the Owl Patrol, your call would mimic the hoot of an owl. This distinctive call is used by the patrol leader to gather the group together and by members to signal their location discreetly. It should be learned by every member, ensuring unity and quick communication within the patrol.

It's important to have someone skilled in imitating animal and bird calls teach the call to the entire patrol. Whether it's the grunt of a bear, the clap of a beaver's tail, the bellow of a bison, the scream of an eagle or hawk, the bark of a fox, the caw of a raven, or any other sound, the call should be recognisable and unique to your patrol.

Upon joining the patrol, new members should learn the call promptly. Remember, in Scouting, each patrol develops its own call, which should never be used by another patrol for any reason.

PATROL CORNERS

The Patrol Corner is a designated space within the Guide Den or outdoors, specifically allocated for patrol activities, meetings, and decorations. It serves as the focal point where the patrol gathers to conduct meetings, plan activities, and display patrol-related materials.

Whether permanent or temporary, the patrol corner embodies the patrol's spirit and identity. It's where Patrol members actively participate in Patrol activities, enhancing their personal development and benefiting both themselves and the community.

Documents and items placed in the patrol corner are engaging and informative, appealing to both Scouts and adult leaders alike, and fostering a sense of learning and camaraderie within the patrol.

HEALTH AND PHYSICAL FITNESS

GENERAL RULES OF HEALTH

Good health is a precious asset, benefiting not just oneself but also the family, community, and nation. It requires knowing and following essential health rules from childhood.

Cleanliness

- **Personal Cleanliness:** Bathe daily or rub down with a cloth, soap, and water if bathing is not possible. Keep your ears and fingernails clean. Wash and comb your hair regularly. Brush teeth in the morning and before bed, and gargle with tepid water and salt at night to prevent infections.

- **Surrounding Cleanliness:** Ensure the living environment is clean and free from dust and dirt. Allow ample sunlight and fresh air into the house. Dispose of waste properly by collecting it in designated bins for municipal collection. In areas without such services, burying waste in pits away from living spaces is advisable. Stagnant water in open drains or pits should be treated with kerosene oil to prevent the breeding of insects like mosquitoes and flies, which carry germs.
- **Mental Cleanliness:** A healthy mind is crucial for overall well-being. Engage in activities that stimulate positive thoughts and emotions, such as reading about great individuals, enjoying art and theatre, and participating in uplifting conversations. Avoid speaking ill of others and strive to understand different viewpoints before forming judgments. Cultivating a positive mindset contributes significantly to mental health.

Exercise

- **Regular Physical Activity:** Engage in regular exercise to maintain physical fitness and health. Exercises should include activities that promote circulation throughout the body and improve muscle strength and flexibility.
- **Outdoor Activities:** Whenever possible, perform exercises outdoors or in well-ventilated areas to benefit from fresh air and natural surroundings.
- **Swimming:** Incorporate swimming into your routine as it provides excellent overall exercise, promoting cardiovascular health and muscular endurance.

Rest

- Adequate rest and sleep are essential for the body and mind to recover and function optimally. Follow a regular sleep schedule and ensure you get enough sleep each night. Also, adhering to the practice of going to bed early and rising early helps maintain a healthy sleep pattern, contributing to overall well-being and productivity.

Food

Food eaten by us is converted by our body into heat and energy, which keep us alive and give us strength to work. We should eat food that supplies our body with the correct ingredients for sustaining our system. Understanding the roles of proteins, carbohydrates, fats, minerals, and vitamins in our diet allows us to make informed choices that significantly impact our health and well-being. By consuming a balanced diet that includes a variety of foods, we ensure an adequate intake of essential nutrients crucial for bodily functions. These are:

- **Proteins:** Proteins are essential for body building and the repair of tissues. They are crucial for the growth and maintenance of muscles, organs, and other tissues.

  Sources: Animal sources include milk, cheese, meat, fish, and eggs. Plant-based sources include dal (lentils), nuts, and green vegetables. Even the outer coats of rice and wheat supply proteins to the body.

- **Carbohydrates:** Carbohydrates are the primary source of energy for the body. They provide fuel for daily activities and support bodily functions.

  Sources: Found abundantly in foods like rice, wheat flour, maize, potatoes, sugar, peas, beans, and carrots. However, excessive carbohydrate intake may lead to flatulence and digestive discomfort.

- **Fats:** Fats are essential for storing energy and insulating organs. They also aid in the absorption of fat-soluble vitamins (like vitamins A, D, E, and K).

  Sources: Butter, ghee, oils, and cream are high in fat content. It's important to consume fat in moderation to maintain a balanced diet and avoid health issues related to excess fat intake.

- **Minerals:** Minerals are vital for various bodily functions, including bone and tooth formation, maintaining fluid balance, and supporting nerve function.

Sources: Calcium, for instance, crucial for bones and teeth, is found in milk and green leafy vegetables. Other minerals like iron, zinc, and potassium are obtained from a variety of foods, including meats, nuts, and vegetables.

- **Vitamins:** Vitamins are essential for growth, immune function, and overall health. They act as antioxidants, help in blood clotting, and support many metabolic processes.

  Sources: Fresh fruits such as tomatoes, citrus fruits (like oranges and lemons), fish, curd, buttermilk, and vegetables like onions, carrots, and turnips are rich in vitamins. It's important to consume these foods to ensure a balanced intake of essential vitamins.

Balancing the intake of proteins, carbohydrates, and fats according to individual needs and activity levels promotes overall health and energy.

Opting for fresh fruits and vegetables enhances our diet by maximising the intake of vitamins and minerals while avoiding overripe, underripe, or exposed-cut fruits, which helps prevent nutrient loss. Hydrating adequately with water supports digestion and overall bodily functions, contributing to optimal health and longevity.

Incorporating these guidelines into our daily eating habits not only nourishes our bodies but also promotes vitality and resilience, ensuring that we maintain a healthy lifestyle for years to come.

Clothing

Wear light and comfortable clothing that allows for ease of movement and does not constrict the body. Regularly wash clothes to maintain cleanliness and hygiene, which is essential for preventing skin infections and promoting overall well-being.

BADEN-POWELL'S SIX EXERCISES

I. **Head Exercise:** Begin by rubbing your head and face firmly with the palms and fingers of both hands. This action stimulates blood circulation and promotes relaxation. Focus on massaging the muscles of the neck and throat using your thumbs, which helps relieve tension and maintain flexibility in these areas.

II. Chest Exercise: Stand upright and bend forward, allowing your arms to stretch downward with the back of your hands together in front of your knees. As you exhale, gradually raise your arms over your head and lean back, inhaling deeply through your nose. Lower your arms slowly to the sides while exhaling through your mouth, saying "Thanks" to complete the breath cycle.

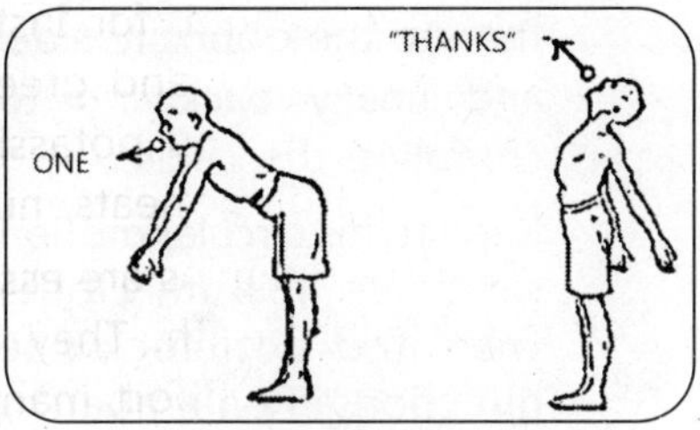

Chest Exercise

Repeat this sequence twelve times to enhance chest flexibility and respiratory capacity.

III. Stomach Exercise (Body Twisting): Stand upright with arms extended straight in front of you, fingers fully extended. Twist your torso slowly to the right from your hips, keeping your feet stationary, and extend your right arm as far behind you as possible. Pause briefly, then twist slowly to the left while inhaling deeply. Coordinate your breathing so that you exhale as you twist to the right and inhale as you twist to the left.

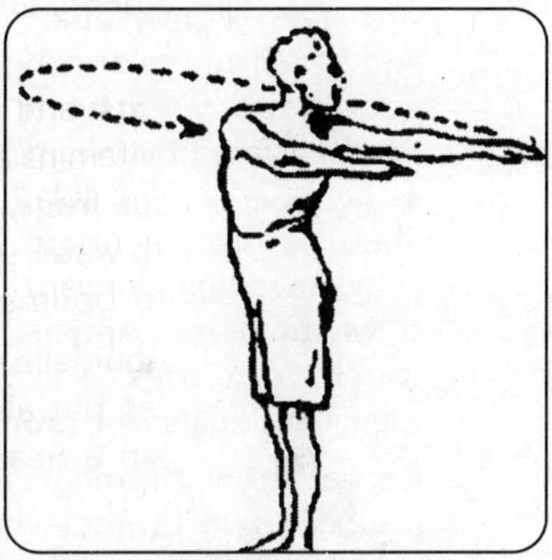
Stomach Exercise

Repeat this twisting movement six times on each side to improve core strength and flexibility.

IV. Trunk Exercise (Cone Exercise): Assume an "attention" position, raising both hands as high as possible above your head and interlocking your fingers. Lean backward and begin to sway your arms in a wide circle above and around your body, pivoting from your hips. Lean to one side, then forward, then to the opposite side, and finally backward to complete the circle.

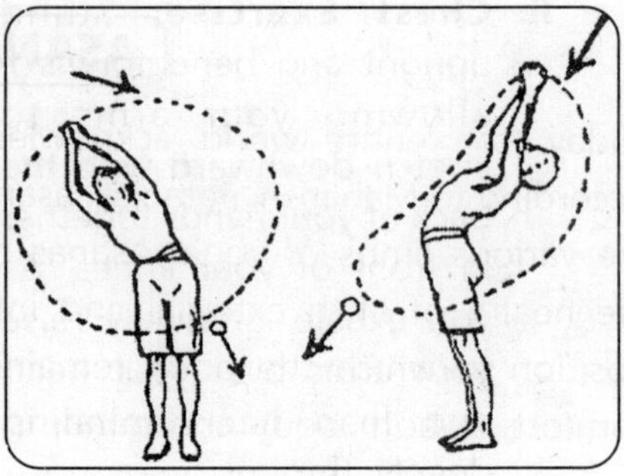

Trunk Exercise

Repeat this circular motion six times in both clockwise and anticlockwise directions. Remember to inhale deeply as you lean backward and exhale as you lean forward, fostering spinal flexibility and core stability.

V. **Lower Body and Back of Legs Exercise:** Stand with your feet slightly apart and reach up to touch your head with both hands, leaning backward as far as is comfortable. Then, without bending your knees, bend forward slowly until your fingers touch your toes. This exercise stretches the lower back and leg muscles.

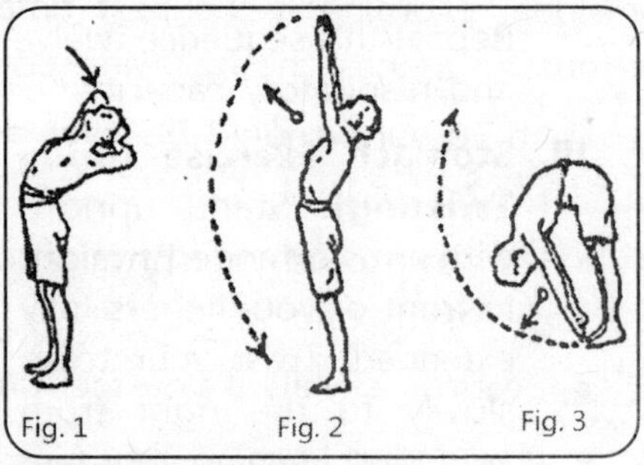

Lower Body Exercise

Repeat this movement twelve times to enhance lower body flexibility and promote hamstring and calf muscle health.

VI. **Legs, Feet, and Toes Exercise:** Begin in the "attention" position with your hands on your hips. Rise onto your tiptoes and turn your knees outward, slowly squatting down while keeping your heels off the ground throughout the movement. Gradually rise back to the starting position.

Repeat this squatting motion twelve times, inhaling as you rise and exhaling as you lower, to strengthen leg muscles and improve ankle flexibility.

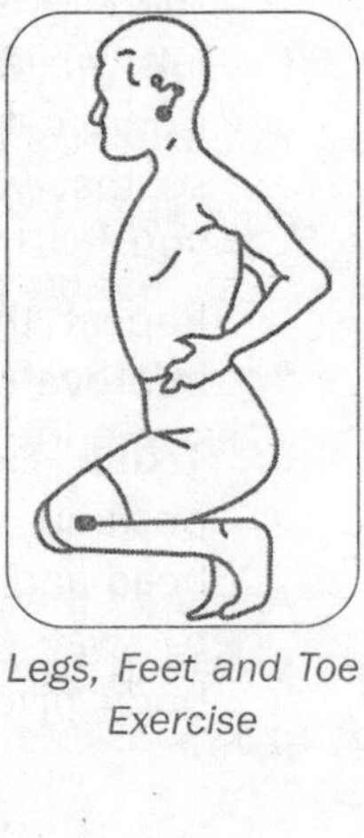

Legs, Feet and Toe Exercise

ASANAS

Today, the entire world acknowledges the importance of yoga. According to Maharishi Patanjali, asanas hold the third position among the various limbs of yoga. Asanas are exercises that help maintain the health of both external and internal organs of the body. Any position in which the body remains stable and at ease, providing comfort to both body and mind, is called an "asana".

Asanas are entirely an Indian exercise technique. They contribute to the physical, mental, intellectual, and spiritual development of an individual. Morning is the best time for practicing asanas. Before performing asanas, the following points should be kept in mind.

- The ground should be level, and a mat or blanket should be placed on it.
- Do not exceed your physical capacity or perform asanas in a diseased condition.
- Rest for a while if you feel tired.
- It is best to practice asanas before taking a bath. If done after bathing, wait at least half an hour.
- Perform asanas only after attending to morning bodily needs.
- Preferably practice asanas in solitude and in an open space. In winter, practice in a well-ventilated room.
- Wear minimal and loose-fitting clothing.
- Initially, perform each asana for a short duration, gradually increasing the duration daily.
- Asanas should be performed under the guidance of a knowledgeable person.
- Always conclude the session with Shavasana (Corpse Pose).

Although there are many asanas, only a few major and simple ones are provided here. For the Pratham Sopan examination, knowledge of any six asanas, based on your interest and need, is required.

SHIRSHASANA (HEADSTAND POSE)

This is one of the most beneficial and well-known asanas. The different stages of this asana are shown in the illustration. Before performing it, place a folded cloth cushion under the head. Initially, while learning, one can take support from a wall. After completing the asana, lower the legs in reverse order and stand straight for a while to restore normal blood circulation.

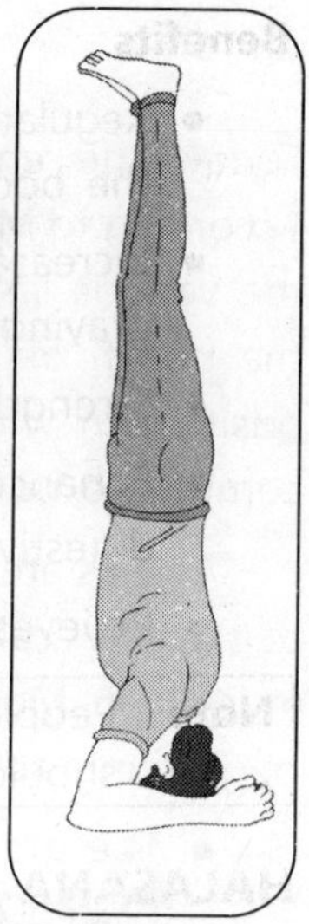

Shirshasana

Benefits

- Strengthens the nervous system, muscles, and digestive organs.
- Enhances brain development and imparts a radiant glow to the face.
- Improves eyesight, prevents premature greying and hair fall.
- Boosts digestion and memory power.

SARVANGASANA (SHOULDER STAND POSE)

Lie flat on the ground with hands close to the body, palms facing down. Slowly lift both legs upwards while exhaling. First, raise the legs up to the waist level and then lift the lower back with the help of both hands, supporting the body to align it in a straight line from shoulders to feet. Try to lift the body as high as possible while keeping the chin tucked into the throat pit. Focus your gaze between the knees. Maintain this position while breathing normally, then slowly lower your legs and release your hands. Relax the body afterward.

Sarvangasana

Benefits

- Regulates heartbeat and improves blood circulation throughout the body.
- Increases appetite, tightens the skin, and prevents premature graying and hair fall.
- Strengthens the liver and spleen.
- Enhances memory, improves facial glow, and helps cure digestive disorders, constipation, and throat diseases.
- Relieves head and eye ailments.

Note: People with high or low blood pressure or heart disease should avoid this asana.

HALASANA (PLOW POSE)

Halasana

Lie flat on your back with your body straight. Slowly raise your legs upwards without bending them while inhaling and then move them over the head to touch the ground with the toes. Hold your breath or exhale slowly while keeping the hips lifted. Bring both hands closer to the head and keep them aligned. After holding for some time, exhale and slowly return to the starting position. Ensure that your knees remain straight throughout the process.

Benefits

- Highly beneficial for diabetes.
- Enhances facial glow and increases body flexibility.
- Reduces fat and energizes the body.
- Helps cure urinary disorders and is beneficial for the abdomen, back, and neck.

MAYURASANA (PEACOCK POSE)

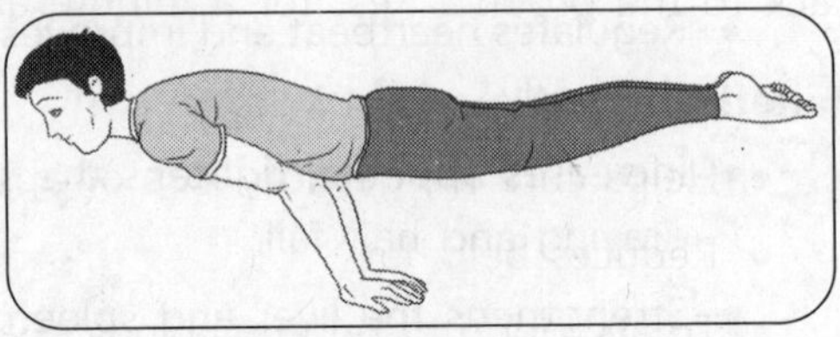
Mayurasana

This asana resembles the shape of a peacock. Sit on the ground on your knees and lean slightly forward. Firmly place your palms on the ground. Gradually bring your stomach onto your elbows and balance your body on them. Stretch your legs straight back. Inhale and lift both legs slightly above the ground, keeping your body parallel to the ground. Maintain this balance for 5-7 seconds and then slowly return to the original position. With practice, this duration can be extended to two minutes. It can also be practiced using the edge of a table for support.

Benefits

- Improves digestion and strengthens the digestive fire, enabling the body to digest anything.
- Enhances the strength of the liver, spleen, stomach, and kidneys.
- Increases energy and vitality.

Note: People with hernia, appendicitis, or intestinal ulcers should avoid this asana.

UTTANPADASANA (RAISED LEGS POSE)

Uttanpadasana

This is considered one of the best asanas for health. Lie flat on your back with your body completely relaxed. Keep your hands close to the thighs and legs together. Slowly inhale and raise your legs while keeping them straight. Contract the abdominal muscles. Hold the position for a short time while holding your breath, then exhale and slowly lower the legs back to the ground. Rest for a minute and repeat the process.

Benefits

- Helps cure indigestion, loss of appetite, and constipation.
- Reduces belly fat.
- Treats blood disorders, jaundice, and headaches.
- Strengthens the body, thighs, abdomen, and pelvic region.

GARUDASANA (EAGLE POSE)

Stand upright. Extend one leg forward and wrap it around the other leg, placing it against the calf. Similarly, wrap both hands around each other and bring them to a prayer position near the nose. Hold for a few seconds and then switch sides.

Garudasana

Benefits

- Strengthens hands and legs.
- Relieves calf pain.
- Highly beneficial for sciatica.

SHAVASANA (CORPSE POSE)

This is the simplest asana among all. Lie down flat on your back with legs slightly apart and hands resting parallel to the body, palms facing down. Relax the entire body completely. Mentally focus on each body part, releasing all tension from feet to head. Breathe naturally and imagine yourself as a lifeless corpse, free from stress and worries.

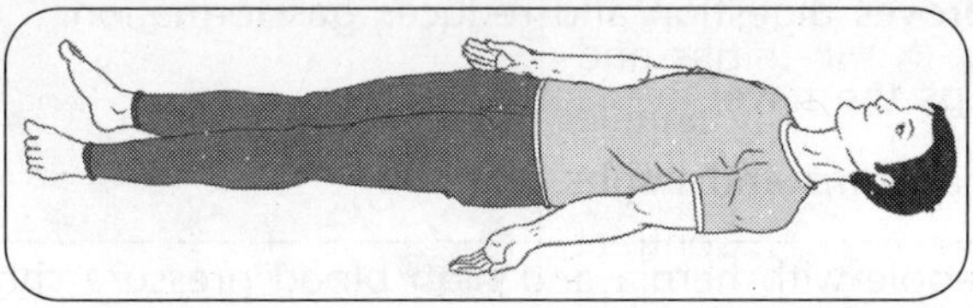

Shavasana

Benefits

- Removes fatigue and makes the body feel light and relaxed.
- Relieves mental stress, bringing happiness and peace of mind.
- Helps overcome depression and frustration.

Note: This asana should be performed for at least three minutes.

DHANURASANA (BOW POSE)

This asana gives the body a bow-like shape. Lie flat on your stomach with legs together. Bend both knees and grasp the ankles with your hands. While exhaling, lift your head and legs upward, pulling the feet as high as possible. Try to take your head backward. Exhale and slowly return to the original position. Repeat multiple times.

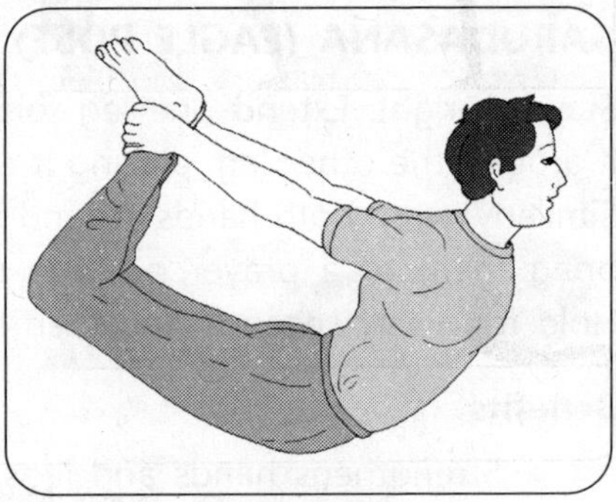

Dhanurasana

Benefits

- Increases flexibility and strengthens the spine.
- Strengthens spinal nerves and muscles.
- Reduces belly fat.
- Alleviates back pain.
- Improves digestion and reduces gas formation.
- Keeps the navel in place.
- Tones arms and thighs.

Note: People with hernia and high blood pressure should avoid this asana.

SURYA NAMASKAR

Surya Namaskar, or Sun Salutation, is a sequence of twelve yoga postures that pay homage to the sun, the ultimate source of energy. Each cycle of Surya Namaskar consists of two sets of these twelve poses, which together form a powerful cardiovascular workout benefiting both mind and body.

Surya Namaskar

- **Step 1: Pranamasana (Prayer Pose):** Begin by standing upright with feet together. Inhale deeply as you raise your arms sideways, expanding your chest, and exhale gently while bringing your palms together in front of your chest. This pose signifies gratitude and sets the intention for the practice.
- **Step 2: Hasta Uttanasana (Raised Arms Pose):** Inhale deeply and lift your arms upward while keeping your palms together. Arch slightly backward to stretch your body and welcome happiness and freedom into your life.
- **Step 3: Hasta Padasana (Hand to Foot Pose):** Exhale slowly as you bend forward from your waist, keeping your spine straight. Focus on folding at the hips while bringing your hands to touch the ground beside your feet. This pose improves digestion and brings balance to the mind.
- **Step 4: Ashwa Sanchalanasana (Equestrian Pose):** Inhale deeply as you stretch your body parallel to the floor. Extend your arms

along your sides and bring your right knee towards the right side of your chest. Arch your back gently and look upward, simultaneously extending your left leg behind you, developing confidence and willpower with the pose.

- **Step 5: Dandasana (Stick Pose):** Inhale and extend your left leg back to align with the right leg, keeping your body parallel to the ground. This pose helps in relaxation and reduces stress.
- **Step 6: Ashtanga Namaskara (Salute with Eight Parts or Points):** Gently lower your knees toward the ground while exhaling deeply. Keep your hips elevated and lower your chin to the ground, maintaining a slight arch in your back. This pose enhances awareness and mindfulness.
- **Step 7: Bhujangasana (Cobra Pose):** Inhale deeply as you lower your hips and arch your back, lifting your chest off the ground while keeping your arms bent. This pose strengthens the back muscles and improves posture.
- **Step 8: Parvatasana (Mountain Pose):** Exhale and raise your hips while keeping your palms and feet in place. This pose stabilises the body and enhances balance.
- **Step 9: Ashwa Sanchalanasana (Equestrian Pose):** Inhale and step your right foot forward between your hands, aligning it with your left foot. This movement continues to build strength and balance.
- **Step 10: Hasta Padasana (Hand to Foot Pose):** Exhale as you bring your left foot forward to meet your right foot, keeping your hands on the ground beside your feet. This pose stretches the back and improves flexibility.
- **Step 11: Hasta Uttanasana (Raised Arms Pose):** Inhale deeply and lift your arms upward, arching backward slightly. This pose expands the chest and improves breathing.
- **Step 12: Pranamasana (Prayer Pose):** Finally, relax your body and exhale while maintaining the Namaskar mudra (prayer position). This completes the cycle with gratitude for the energy and benefits gained from the practice.

COMMUNICATION AND SIGNALLING

HAND SIGNALS

Hand signals play a crucial role in scouting, serving as silent communication tools that patrol leaders can use effectively, especially in situations where verbal communication is impractical or unnecessary. These signals, also known as silent signs, are essential during activities such as hikes, handling confidential matters, or when maintaining silence is critical. These signs have an important place in the discipline system of the unit. These are very interesting international signs.

1. **Horizontal Wave across Face or Flag:** This gesture, where the hand or flag is waved several times horizontally across the face or opposite the face, signifies messages such as "No,""Never mind," or "As you were."
2. **Slow Vertical Wave with Hand or Flag Held High:** When the hand or flag is held high and waved slowly from side to side at full arm extension, it indicates commands like "Extend,""Go farther out," or "Scatter."
3. **Quick Vertical Wave with Hand or Flag Held High:** This rapid waving motion with the hand or flag held high at full arm extension signifies instructions to "Close in," "Rally," or "Come here."
4. **Pointing Hand or Flag in Any Direction:** Simply pointing with the hand or flag indicates the direction to move or proceed.
5. **Clenched Fist or Flag Jumped Rapidly Up and Down:** A clenched fist or rapidly jumping flag signals "Run" or "Hurry."
6. **Hand or Flag Held Straight Up Overhead:** Holding the hand or flag straight up overhead signifies "Stop" or "Halt."

These hand signals are standardised internationally and are vital for maintaining order, safety, and discipline during Scout activities.

WHISTLE SIGNALS

Whistle signals are another essential means of communication in Scouting, particularly useful when Scouts are within hearing distance, but vocal commands might be impractical or too disruptive. Some common whistle signals are:

1. **One Long Blast:** Signals "Silence," "Alert," or "Lookout for my next signal."
2. **Succession of Long, Slow Blasts:** Indicates commands like "Go out," "Get further away," "Advance," or "Scatter."
3. **Succession of Long, Sharp Blasts:** Signals instructions to "Rally," "Close in," "Come together," or "Fall in."
4. **Alternating Long and Short Blasts:** Used for urgent messages like "Alarm," "Look out," "Be ready," or "Man your alarm posts."
5. **Three short blasts followed by one long blast:** Specifically calls up the patrol leader, indicating, "Leaders come in here."
6. **Two short blasts, followed by one long blast:** Call up the duty patrol leader to attend to a specific matter.

These whistle signals are standardised and widely used in Scouting to ensure effective coordination, response, and safety during field activities and exercises.

Understanding and practicing these signals is fundamental for scouts and leaders to maintain cohesion, efficiency, and safety in various scouting scenarios.

Whistle signals have two kinds of call long blast and short blast.

Long blast : –

Short blast : •

SIGNALS	MEANING
—	Silence, Caution for next commands.
— — — — —	Scatter, Advance, Go away
• — • — • —	Alarm, Look out, Be ready
• • • • • •	Come together, fall in, Come Come.

WOODCRAFT AND OUTDOOR SKILLS

WOODCRAFT SIGNS AND FOLLOWING A TRAIL

Trail signs are essential for guiding scouts along paths, especially in situations where verbal communication isn't feasible, such as during hikes or in noisy environments. They are crucial for maintaining order within the scout group and ensuring everyone stays on the correct route without confusion. Trail signs are typically made from natural materials like sticks, pebbles, or twigs. These materials are chosen to blend with the surroundings yet remain visible. Signs are placed on the right-hand side of the trail to ensure consistency and are positioned close to the ground, no higher than knee level. This positioning ensures they are easily seen but not obstructive.

Signs are kept small, approximately the size of a hand, to maintain clarity without drawing unnecessary attention. This size also makes them easy to handle and place discreetly along the trail. Visibility is key, ensuring that even in varying light conditions, the signs can be spotted by scouts following the trail.

Types and Meanings of Signs

1. **Small Arrow:** Indicates the direction of the trail, guiding scouts forward along the designated path.
2. **'X' Symbol:** Placed where trails might intersect or where a wrong path could be mistaken. It signals scouts to avoid that direction.
3. **Numbered Square with Arrow:** Indicates a message has been hidden in the indicated direction, with the number of paces away specified.
4. **A circle with a dot:** Marks the end of a trail or signifies that the trail leader has returned home.

Best Practices for Following a Trail

- **Attention to Detail:** Scouts are trained to follow trail signs attentively. They are instructed to verify each sign they encounter to ensure it's a genuine marker and not an accidental formation in nature.

- **Backtracking:** If a sign is missed or misunderstood, scouts are encouraged to backtrack to the last recognised marker and resume from there to prevent getting lost or leading others astray.
- **Erasing Signs:** Erasing or removing trail signs after completing the trail is emphasized. This practice ensures that future scout groups or individuals won't be confused by outdated markers, maintaining the integrity of the trail for all users. It also teaches scouts responsibility and respect for the environment.

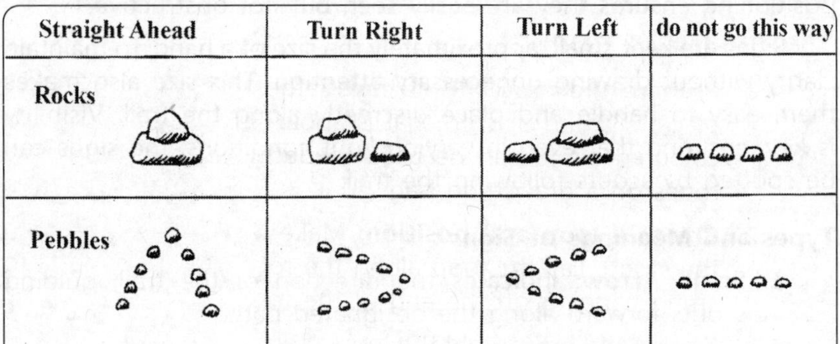

Trail Signs

Advancing to Indian Trail Signs

Scouts may advance to learning Indian trail signs, which involve more intricate methods such as arranging stones, tying grass into knots, or placing sticks in specific patterns. These signs provide additional skills for effective navigation and communication on trails, enriching the scouting experience with cultural and practical knowledge.

Trail signs are an integral part of scouting, teaching valuable skills in navigation, observation, and environmental stewardship. By mastering these signs, scouts become more adept at leading and following trails, ensuring safety and organisation during outdoor activities.

WHIPPING A ROPE

1. **Prepare the rope and string:** Gather a piece of rope and a piece of string or cord that is about 12 inches long. Brightly coloured string can be used to decorate the jump rope or ropes on a drawstring bag.
2. **Create a loop and position:** Make a loop with one end of the string. Lay the loop along the rope with the ends of the string hanging off the end of the rope.
3. **Secure the loop:** Hold the loop in place with your left thumb. This loop will be the starting point for wrapping the string around the rope.
4. **Wrap the string around the rope:** With your right hand, begin winding the long end of the string tightly over the loop and around the rope. Wind the string around the rope for at least an inch, ensuring that each wrap is firm and close but not overlapping.
5. **Continue Wrapping:** Wind the string firmly and closely around the rope, ensuring it stays in place. As you wind, the short end of the string will be left hanging.
6. **Secure the end:** When you have wound the string for a sufficient length (about an inch or more), tuck the end of the string that you've been winding through the loop. Hold this end with your left thumb to prevent it from loosening.

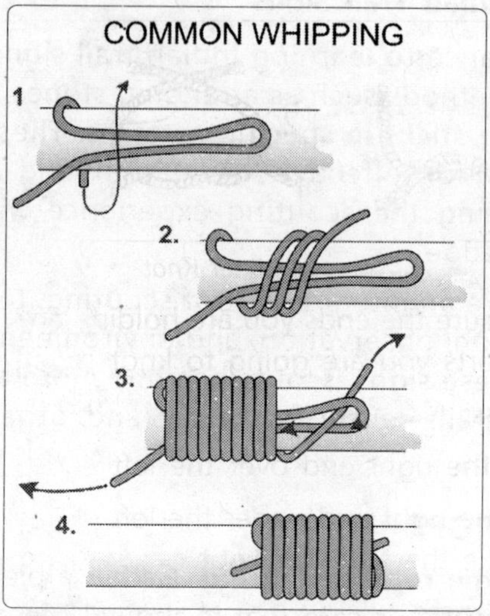

7. **Finish the whipping:** Take the remaining end of the string and pull it slowly. As you pull, the loop will disappear under the winding. Continue pulling until the loop is halfway under the winding.
8. **Trim the ends:** Once the loop is secured under the winding, trim the ends of the string to make a neat finish. This ensures that the whipping is tidy and won't unravel easily.
9. **Check the tightness:** If the whipping slips off the rope, it means it wasn't wound tightly enough. Practice until the whipping holds firmly when you try to push it off.

KNOTS AND ITS TYPES

REEF KNOT

A reef knot, also known as a square knot, is a simple and secure knot used for joining two ends of a rope together.

Step-by-Step Instructions

1. **Position the ropes:**
   - Hold one end of a rope in your right hand and the other end in your left hand.

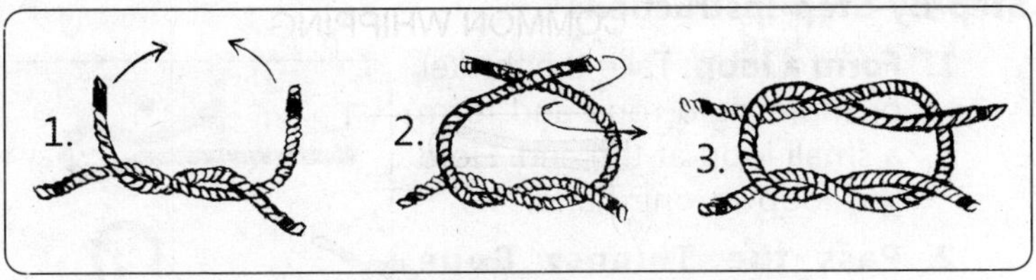

Reef Knot

- Make sure the ends you are holding are the working ends (the parts you are going to knot together).

2. **First Cross:**
   - Cross the right end over the left end.
   - Tuck the right end under the left end and pull it through to make the first-half knot.
3. **Second Cross:**
   - Cross the left end over the right end.
   - Tuck the left end under the right end and pull it through to make the second-half knot.
4. **Tighten the knot:** Pull both ends of the rope to tighten the knot.

   Ensure the knot lies flat and snug, with no twists.
5. **Check the Knot:** Verify that the knot looks like two loops linked together.

   It should resemble a square or box-like shape.

Uses: This knot is employed to join two ends of ropes that are of the same thickness. It is also recommended for securing triangular bandages. Additionally, it serves well for fastening parcels or tying ropes around bundles of bedding, as commonly done by dholbus. This knot lies flat, prevents slipping, and can be untied with ease.

SHEET BEND

A sheet bend is a versatile knot used for joining two ropes of different thicknesses or types. Sailors call some of the ropes used on sails "sheets." A "bend" is a way of making a loop.

Step-by-Step Instructions

1. **Form a loop:** Take the thicker or more rigid rope and form a small loop at the end. Hold the loop in one hand.
2. **Pass the Thinner Rope Through the Loop:** Take the thinner or more flexible rope and pass its end up through the loop from underneath (from the back of the loop towards the front).
3. **Wrap Around the Loop:** Bring the end of the thinner rope around the back of the loop and then pass it back under itself where it initially came through the loop.

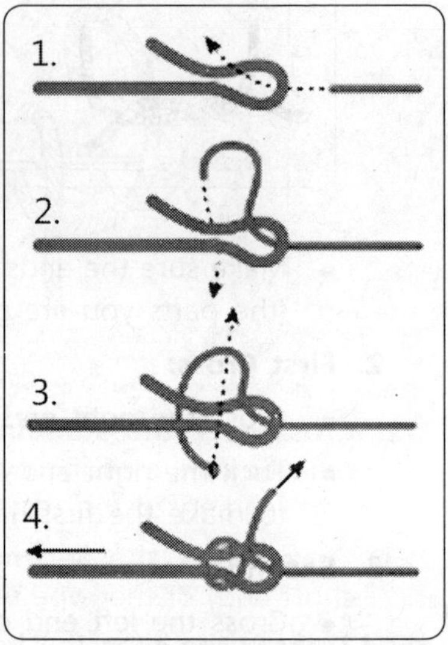

Sheet Bend

4. **Tighten the knot:** Pull both the standing end (the part of the rope leading to the rest of the rope) and the working end (the short end) of the thinner rope to tighten the knot. Make sure the knot is snug and secure.

Uses: This knot is suitable for joining ropes of unequal thickness and for attaching a rope to a loop or joining ropes to materials like staffs, sails, or cloth. The loops should be formed in the material or thick rope. It is commonly used for hoisting flags. This knot is practical when only short lengths of rope are available.

CLOVE HITCH

The clove hitch is a simple and effective knot used for securing a rope to a post, pole, or other object.

Step-by-Step Instructions

1. **Wrap around the object:** Take the rope and make a turn around the object (e.g., a pole or tree branch) from left to right.

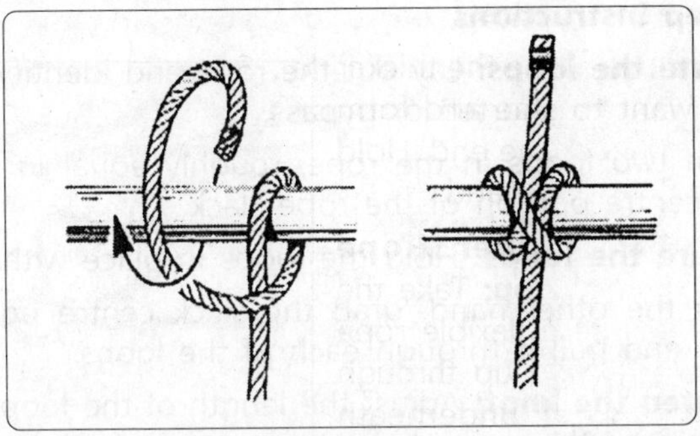

Clove-Hitch

2. **Cross over the standing part:** Bring the rope around the object again, crossing over the standing part of the rope (the part leading to the rest of the rope).
3. **Tuck Under the Second Turn:** Tuck the working end (the short end) of the rope under the second turn you just made.
4. **Tighten the knot:** Pull both the standing end and the working end of the rope to tighten the knot securely around the object.

Uses: This knot is ideal for fastening one end of a rope around a post or tree, setting up a clothesline or a badminton net, and for starting lashing. It is not suitable for securing moving objects like animals because the motion can loosen the hitch. This knot is particularly useful when you cannot cut the rope or access its ends easily. It can also be employed to support a weak section of rope under strain. In household applications, it's handy for adjusting the height of a hanging electric lamp cord.

SHEEP SHANK

The sheep shank is a knot used to temporarily shorten a rope or take slack out of a line. It's particularly useful in situations where you need to quickly adjust the length of a rope without cutting it.

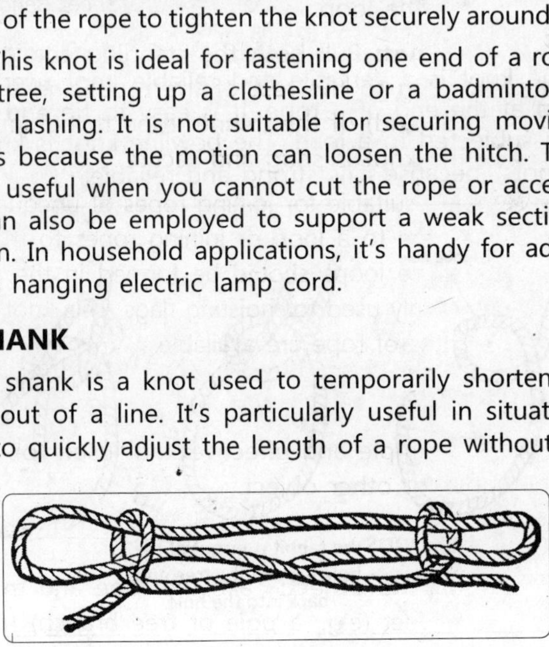

Sheep Shank

Step-by-Step Instructions

1. **Create the loops:** Lay out the rope and identify the section you want to shorten or bypass.

   Form two loops in the rope, roughly equal in size, leaving the centre portion of the rope slack.

2. **Secure the loops:** Hold the loops in place with one hand.

   With the other hand, grab the slack centre portion of the rope and pull it through each of the loops.

3. **Tighten the knot:** Adjust the length of the loops as needed to achieve the desired shortening or bypass.

   Pull all parts of the knot snugly to secure it.

Uses: It's commonly used to temporarily shorten a rope that is too long for a specific task. It can be used to bypass a damaged section of rope to prevent further unravelling or to isolate the damaged part. The sheep shank knot is handy in situations where you need to quickly adjust rope length or bypass damaged sections, providing a practical solution in various outdoor, marine, and survival contexts.

BOWLINE

The bowline knot is a versatile and reliable knot used to form a secure loop at the end of a rope. It is easy to tie and untie, even after being subjected to a load. The bowline knot is known as the "King of Knots" because it is strong and reliable.

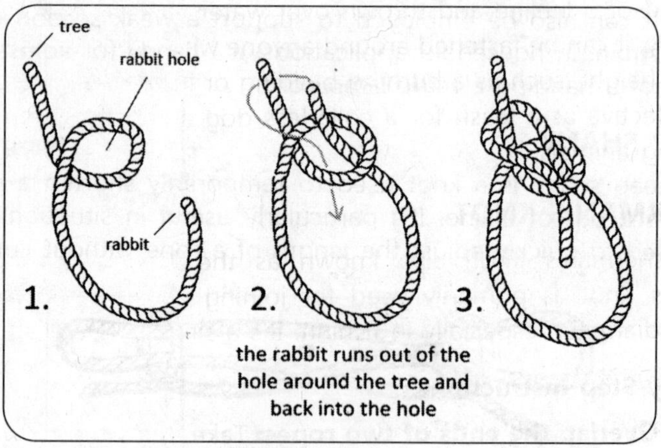

Bowling Knot

Step-by-Step Instructions

1. **Form a Loop:** Take the rope and create a large loop by folding the working end over the standing part (the long section of the rope). The working end should be on top of the standing part.
2. **Thread the Working End:** Pass the working end of the rope through the loop from underneath. The working end should come up through the loop, away from the standing part.
3. **Create the Second Loop:** Take the working end and bring it around the back of the standing part, forming a second loop.
4. **Finish the Knot:** Pull the working end back through the original loop you created in step 1. The working end should now be coming back towards you, creating a large loop at the end of the rope.
5. **Tighten the Knot:** Hold the knot in one hand and pull the standing part and the working end in opposite directions to tighten the knot. Make sure the knot is snug and the loop is the desired size.

Uses: This knot creates a loop that is secure and does not slip, making it highly valuable in rescue operations. It is typically tied at one end of a lifeline and thrown over water to a drowning person. Similarly, it can be fastened around anyone who needs to be lowered from a height, such as a burning building or into a well. This knot is also effective as a leash for a collarless dog and is commonly used for tying animals.

FISHERMAN'S KNOT

The Fisherman's Knot, also known as the Fisherman's Bend or Angler's Knot, is primarily used for joining two ropes or lines of similar diameter, especially in fishing. It's a simple and reliable knot.

Step-by-Step Instructions

1. **Overlap the ends of two ropes:** Take the two ropes or lines you want to join and overlap their ends for a few inches.

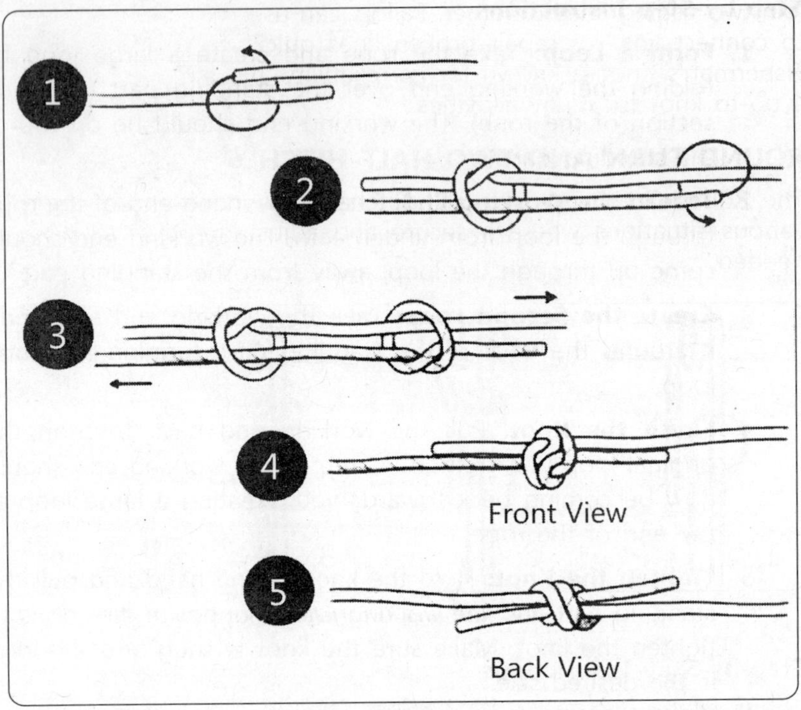

Fisherman's Knot

2. **Tie the first overhand knot:** Using the end of one rope, tie a simple overhand knot around the standing part of the other rope. Pull it snug, but not too tight.
3. **Tie the second overhand knot:** Now, using the end of the other rope, tie another overhand knot around the standing part of the first rope. Again, pull it snug but not too tight.
4. **Pull the Knots Together:** Hold the standing parts of both ropes and pull them apart. This will slide the two overhand knots together.
5. **Tighten the knots:** Pull both knots tightly to secure the Fisherman's Knot. The two overhand knots will jam against each other, creating a strong connection.

Uses: This knot is used for tying two wet or slippery ropes. The primary use of the Fisherman's Knot is in fishing. It is used to join two fishing lines together. Sailors can use the Fisherman's Knot to connect lines or repair broken lines quickly and efficiently. The Fisherman's Knot is known for its reliability and strength, making it a go-to knot for many activities.

ROUND TURN AND TWO HALF-HITCHES

The Round Turn and Two Half Hitches is a versatile knot used in various situations where a secure and adjustable loop or hitch is needed.

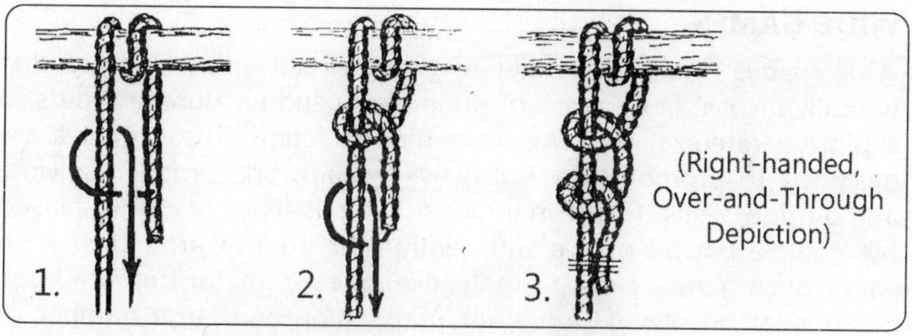

Round Turn and Two Half-Hitches

Step-by-Step Instructions

1. **Make a round turn:** Start by wrapping the working end of the rope around the object (such as a pole or post) where you want to secure it. This wrap is known as a "round turn." Ensure that the rope crosses over itself as it wraps around the object.
2. **First Half Hitch:** After making the round turn, take the working end of the rope and pass it under the standing part (the part of the rope that runs directly from the knot towards the spool or other anchor point).

   Bring the working end over the top of the standing part.
3. **Second Half Hitch:** Repeat the process of passing the working end under the standing part.

   This time, bring the working end over the top and through the loop created in the previous step.

   Pull the working end tight to secure the knot.

Uses: This knot is also used to attach a rope to a pole or a tree. It is safe, no matter in what direction the pull comes. So it is suitable for tying up a boat or an animal. This knot is commonly used in boating and sailing to secure ropes to cleats or other objects on board. It's useful for securing tarpaulin, tents, and other camping gear to trees or poles.

TROOP GAMES AND DRILLS

WIDE GAMES

Wide games in scouting refer to outdoor activities or games that typically involve large areas of open space and encourage scouts to explore, strategize, and work together as teams. These games are designed to promote physical activity, teamwork, problem-solving, and outdoor skills. The term indicates various types of games played by multiple patrols over a sufficiently wide area of ground or even water. Such games can be simple, like an easy trail or treasure hunt, or complex, involving significant preparation and large number of scouts from different troops.

In the early days of scouting, such games were commonly known as Field Days, a term with military significance that still captures the essence of the activity–a day spent in the fields and woods. The original edition of Scouting for Boys featured games like "Scout Meets Scout,""Despatch Runners," and "Lion Hunting," which were highly popular. "Flag Raiding," a game from Aids to Scout Tag written by Baden Powell or B.P. before the South African War, became one of the most popular wide games.

Key Aspects of Wide Games

- **Clarity and preparation:** If a wide game is to be successful, it must be understood by all participants. Discuss the game in the Court of Honour and ensure that patrol leaders know exactly what is expected of them. It is a good idea to take the patrol leaders over the ground where the game will be played.
- **Simplicity and Structure:** Keep the games as simple as possible. If two sides are to meet in opposition, ensure that they do. Have a clear means of starting and finishing the game, such as the firing of a rocket or the use of gas rattles.

- **Lives System:** Use a system where each scout ties a piece of wool above the elbow, with different colours for each team. "Dead" scouts can get a new life from an umpire by paying a forfeit, like answering a scout test question or tying a knot.
- **Scoring and Feedback:** At the conclusion of the game, umpires award marks for the number of lives captured, achievement of objectives, etc., and declare the winner. The umpire might give a short summary of the results, pointing out faults and giving praise where due.
- **Conclusion and Reflection:** The final proceedings could include tea and a campfire, providing an opportunity for reflection and camaraderie.

Wide games are an integral part of scouting activities, providing memorable experiences that blend adventure with learning, teamwork, and skill development in natural settings.

Examples of Wide Games

1. **Capture the Flag:** A classic wide game where teams try to capture each other's flag from their base without being tagged.
2. **Manhunt:** Scouts try to evade capture while navigating through a designated area, often involving stealth and strategy.
3. **Survival Scenario:** Simulates survival situations where teams must find food, water, and shelter while navigating challenges in the wilderness.
4. **Pioneering Challenges:** This involves building structures such as bridges, towers, or shelters using ropes and pioneering skills.
5. **Treasure Hunt:** Teams follow clues or a map to locate hidden treasures or complete a series of tasks.

Wide games provide a dynamic and engaging way for scouts to apply their skills in real-world scenarios, fostering a spirit of adventure and cooperation.

XYZ GAME

For each patrol, the game requires an X object, a set of Y cards, and several Z objects. Patrol Leaders (P.L.s) are informed of the game area and the exact time they need to report to one of several umpires positioned within the area. This designated time marks the start of the game. Each P.L. receives an envelope from an umpire containing the X object, which allows their patrol to participate, along with several Y cards that will be distributed among patrol members. The patrols have three main tasks:

1. **Collect Y Cards:** Patrol members must search for scouts from other patrols to gather as many Y cards as possible. The Y cards can be hidden anywhere on a scout's person, but any scout who is touched on the back and given the password (the name of the X object) must submit to being searched. The searching scout can then take all the Y cards found on the other scout. It allows the searcher to escape quickly after collecting the cards.
2. **Report Suspicious Characters:** Scouts need to observe and report any suspicious characters within a specific sub-area during certain hours. This task helps improve their observation and reporting skills and brings competing patrols into closer interaction, increasing the game's excitement.
3. **Collect Z Objects:** After a certain period, patrols must collect as many Z objects as they can from designated places such as hedges, ditches, walls, or gardens. These objects should be camouflaged but not completely hidden. Patrols must first report to an umpire, identifiable by a blue flower or similar marker, before they start searching for Z objects. This brings the patrols together as the game progresses towards its end.

P.L.s are informed of the game's ending time and are given a few minutes to return to headquarters to submit their collected X, Y, and Z objects. Ideally, the activity concludes with a grand tea, providing an enjoyable and rewarding finish to an exhilarating afternoon.

LIGHT THAT LAMP

The premise of this game, perfect for a Saturday afternoon or as an idea for future camps, revolves around a lighthouse keeper who, on a stormy night, finds himself out of fuel for his lamp. He sends an urgent radio message to the shore for more fuel, which is then sent via an aerial railway because the sea is too rough for a boat. Thankfully, the fuel arrives just in time to prevent a ship from crashing on the rocks.

Before the game starts, each patrol sets up an aerial railway by stretching a length of rope between trees or from a slope's top to the bottom. A bucket is attached to each rope handle, with sisal cord lines for pulling it along.

The game begins with one end of the rope representing the lighthouse and the other the top of the cliffs, with the sea in between, which must not be crossed. The Patrol Leaders (P.L.s) act as lighthouse keepers, while the other scouts play the coastguards. The objective for each P.L. is to light a fire, but all the necessary materials, including fuel, paper, and matches, must be sent to them in the bucket.

It becomes a race to see which lighthousekeeper can light their lamp within a set time, such as fifteen minutes. At the end of this period, a ship (represented by the Scout Master, or S.M.) arrives, and ten points are awarded for each lit lamp. The buckets must be sent back and forth continuously to maintain the fuel supply until the ship arrives, creating excitement and amusement, especially when sticks fall out mid-way. If the rope's angle is steep enough, a push should suffice to send the bucket down; otherwise, on a level setup between two trees, a double line will be needed to haul it both ways.

SPIES AMONG US

Two teams start from points about 500 yards apart. Each participant receives half of a message written on a slip of paper. The goal is for members of each team to find someone from the other team with the missing half of their message. However, before they can compare notes, each participant must give a prearranged sign to indicate they are willing to "risk" the exchange. This is a risk because there is a spy on each team.

Instead of having half of a message, the spies' slips of paper simply say "Spy." If a participant agrees to compare notes with a spy from the opposing team, they must hand over their slip of paper to the spy and return to a designated base without revealing the spy's identity to others. The first pair to return to the base with a complete and coherent message wins the game.

DRILL COMMANDS

- **Fall In:** All patrols line up in a single row in front of the scout master. Occasionally, formations of two or three lines may be used.
- **Right Dress:** The scout at the right end of the front line stands still. The scouts directly behind him adjust their distance to thirty inches and align themselves properly, keeping their eyes forward. All other scouts in the front rank turn their heads and eyes to the right and raise their right arm with a clenched fist. Scouts holding a staff will use their left arm. Scouts in the second or third lines adjust their alignment by looking to the right without raising their arms.
- **Eyes Front:** When the command "Eyes Front" is given, everyone turns their head and eyes back to the front and lowers their arm smartly.
- **Left Dress:** Perform the same actions as "Right Dress," but substitute "left" for "right" throughout.
- **Stand-at-Ease:** Move the left foot to the side about twelve inches. Maintain a balanced posture with hands behind the back, right palm resting on the left hand, fingers extended, and thumbs crossed. No movement is allowed until "Stand Easy" is commanded. You can relax, but you must not move your feet or talk.
- **Attention:** Bring the left foot back to the right, stand straight with your head and eyes forward, arms at your sides with your hands closed, and thumbs pointing forward just behind the seams of your trousers. Keep heels together and toes apart.

- **Right Turn:**
  - At the halt, pivot on the right heel and left toe, bringing the left foot to meet the right.
  - **On the Move:** The command is given as the right foot is passing the left. Complete the turn with the left foot and resume marching with the right foot.
- **Left Turn:** Reverse the instructions given for the right turn, substituting "left" for "right."
- **About Turn:**
  - **At the Halt:** Similar to the right turn but involves turning 180 degrees.
  - **On the Move:** The command is given as the left foot is passing the right. Complete the turn with the left foot and march off with the right foot on the fourth beat. Check your alignment by counting one, two, three and then right-left.
- **Number:** The front rank numbers are off from the right side.
- **Open and Close Orders March:** Take two short paces, stepping off with the left foot. The front rank moves forward, while the rear rank moves backward.
- **Dismiss:** Turn to the right, salute, lift your heels, and then disperse.

FIRST AID

UNDERSTANDING FIRST AID

First aid involves the initial care given to someone who is injured or suddenly becomes ill, with the goal of preserving life, preventing the condition from worsening, and aiding recovery until professional medical assistance is available. This may include basic procedures like applying bandages, performing CPR (cardiopulmonary resuscitation), managing shock, and stabilising injuries.

The individual providing first aid is known as a "first aider." Their responsibility concludes once professional medical help is on the scene. To deliver effective first aid, a first aider should follow the mnemonic FIRST AID:

F = **First Aid:** Administer immediate care to the injured or ill person.

I = **Investigation (Observation):** Assess the situation and identify the nature of the injury or illness.

R = **Resourceful:** Utilise available resources to prevent further harm or injury.

S = **sympathetic:** Offer comfort and reassurance to the affected individual.

T = **Tactful:** Approach the situation with sensitivity, gathering information about symptoms without causing additional distress.

A = **Assistance, ambulance:** Seek help from others trained in first aid or call for an ambulance if needed.

I = **Immediate:** Act swiftly, especially in cases of serious injury or medical emergencies.

D = **Doctor:** Ensure that the patient receives further evaluation and treatment from a medical professional.

A first aider is not a substitute for a doctor and should not attempt to provide medical treatment beyond their training. Their primary role is to offer initial support and care until professional help can take over.

CONTENTS OF A FIRST AID BOX

1. **Gauze Pieces:** Cut into 4″ by 1 ½″ size, packed in polythene bags, sealed, and sterilised in a pressure cooker. There should be at least 10 such bags in your kit.
2. **Bandages:**
    - ❑ **Rolled Bandages:** Made from unbleached cloth, cut into strips 4′ wide and 2 metres long. There should be at least 8 rolls in your kit.
    - ❑ **Triangular Bandages:** Cut from a square cloth measuring 40 inches along the diagonal. Pad and sterilise each bandage separately. Have at least 4 triangular bandages in your kit.
3. **Adhesive Plaster:** A roll of 3′ wide adhesive plaster and 2 dozen Band-Aid strips in various sizes and shapes.

4. **Elastic Crepe Bandage:** 4′ wide.
5. **Scissors and tweezers:** one pair of each.
6. **Dettol:** A bottle.
7. **Soframycine Cream:** A tube.
8. **Thick Gauze Pad:** Packed in polythene and sterilized. Have at least three such packets.
9. **Common salt:** Some amount.
10. **Safety Pins:** Several.

These items are essential for a comprehensive first aid kit, covering a range of common injuries and emergencies.

USE OF ROLLER BANDAGES AND TRIANGULAR BANDAGES

ROLLER BANDAGES

Roller bandages are versatile tools in first aid, used for various purposes such as holding dressings in place, applying pressure to control bleeding, and providing support to injured limbs or joints. A guide on how to apply roller bandages effectively is as following:

Choosing the Right Bandage

- **Bandage Width:** Select the appropriate width based on the body part being bandaged.
  - **Lower arm, elbow, hand, and foot:** 75 mm (3 inches).
  - **Upper arm, knee, and lower leg:** 100 mm (4 inches).
  - **Large leg or trunk:** 150 mm (6 inches).
- **Material:** Choose between lightweight cotton for holding dressings and crepe or elasticised crepe for applying support or firm pressure.

Application Steps

- **Prepare the Patient:** Ensure the injured part is adequately supported and positioned comfortably.

- **Starting the Bandage:**
  - ❑ Hold the tightly rolled bandage with the 'head' (start) of the bandage on top.
  - ❑ Begin wrapping the 'tail' (end) around the body part, ensuring not to unroll more than a few centimetres at a time.
- **Locking Turn:**
  - ❑ Begin with a locking turn to secure the start of the bandage under each subsequent turn. This helps to prevent it from unravelling.
- **Wrapping Technique:**
  - ❑ Start from the middle of the body or limb, working outward.
  - ❑ Begin at the narrowest part below the dressing or injury site and work upwards.
  - ❑ Each turn should cover about two-thirds of the previous turn, ensuring even and secure coverage.
  - ❑ Completely cover any dressing or padding used to protect the wound.
- **Finishing the Bandage:**
  - ❑ Finish with a straight turn at the end of the bandage.
  - ❑ Secure the bandage with a safety pin or adhesive tape. Avoid using metal clips, as they may be less secure and can come loose during movement.

Specific Applications

- **Lower Arm or Leg:**
  - ❑ Apply a dressing or padding over the affected area.
  - ❑ Start with a diagonal locking turn below the dressing, then continue upward, covering two-thirds of each previous turn.
  - ❑ Finish with a straight turn and secure.
- **Elbow or knee:**
  - ❑ Apply a dressing or padding.
  - ❑ Begin with a full turn over the point of the elbow or knee to secure the bandage.

- ❑ Make subsequent turns above and below the joint, alternating to avoid excessive pressure.
- ❑ Finish with a full turn above the joint and secure.

- **Hand or foot:**
  - ❑ Apply a dressing or padding.
  - ❑ Start with a diagonal locking turn around the wrist or foot.
  - ❑ Continue with turns across the back of the hand or foot, working upwards to cover the dressing.
  - ❑ Finish with a circular turn around the wrist or ankle and secure.

By following these steps, one can effectively apply roller bandages to provide support, control bleeding, and protect wounds, ensuring comfort and stability for the injured person.

TRIANGULAR BANDAGES

The triangular bandage is a versatile tool in first aid, used for various applications due to its shape and size.

Construction of Triangular Bandages

Made from a piece of linen or calico, it is at least 38 inches square.

- Diagonally cut into two pieces to form two triangular bandages.
- Each bandage has three borders: one longest, called the "base," and two shorter sides. It also has three corners: one upper (opposite the base) called the "point," and two lower corners called the "ends."

Application of Triangular Bandages:

- **As a Whole Cloth:** Spread out to its full extent, used for large areas like chest bandages.
- **As a Broad Bandage:** Fold the point down to the centre of the base, then fold again in the same direction to create a broad strip.
- **As a Narrow Bandage:** Further fold the broad bandage once again in the same direction to create a narrower strip.

- Optionally, the bandage can be halved by bringing the two ends together before folding into a broad or narrow bandage.

Securing with a Reef Knot:

- A reef knot (square knot) is used to secure the ends of the bandage.
- Cross the ends: right over left, then left over right, ensuring it is snug but not tight.
- Place the knot where it doesn't cause discomfort or chafe the skin, and tuck the ends away to secure it.

Applying Triangular Bandages

Arm Sling:

- Encourage the patient to hold the affected arm across the body.
- Place the bandage with the base running down the centre of the body and the point towards the elbow of the affected side.
- Pass the top point under the supported arm, wrap it around the back of the neck, and let it rest on the shoulder of the affected side.
- Lift the lower point to meet the upper point at the side of the neck.

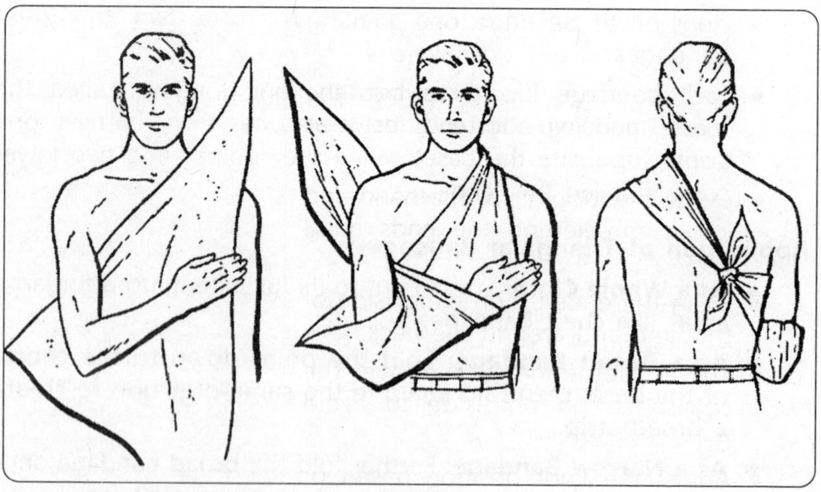

Arm Sling

- Tie a reef knot just above the collarbone, ensuring no pressure on the neck.
- Adjust the sling so fingertips are visible, and secure the point with a safety pin.

Elevation Sling:

- Encourage the patient to hold the affected arm across the body with fingers pointing to the opposite shoulder.
- Position the bandage with the base down in the centre and the point at the elbow of the affected side.
- Place the bandage over the supported arm, and carry the top end around the neck to rest on the unaffected shoulder.
- Wrap the lower half of the bandage along the affected arm and across the back.
- Twist the top point around the fingers gently, avoiding pressure on the injury.
- Tie a reef knot above the collarbone, adjusting for comfort and safety.

Collar-and-Cuff Sling:

- Make a clove hitch with two large loops of the bandage, one pointing upwards and one downwards.
- Fold the loops inward towards the middle, trapping both ends between them.
- Guide the loops over the hand and lower arm, letting the ends hang down.
- Bring the ends up on either side of the limb and around the neck.
- Tie a reef knot just above the collarbone on one side to avoid neck pressure.

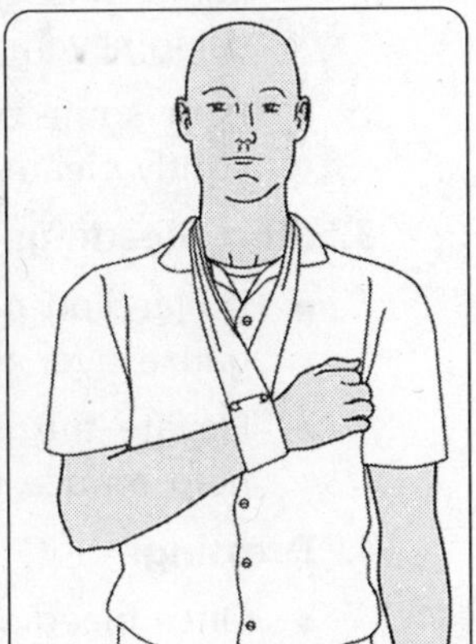

Collar and Cuff Sling

- Adjust the knot position based on the injury location and patient comfort.

Folding and Storage:

- When not in use, fold the triangular bandage into a narrow shape.
- Fold the two ends to the centre, then fold the bandage to the centre again.
- Finally, fold it in half to create a compact packet, approximately 6.5 inches by 3.5 inches in size, for easy storage and quick access.

These bandages can also be improvised from various materials, like handkerchiefs, belts, or other fabrics, in emergency situations, making them versatile tools in first aid kits.

CUTS AND SCRATCHES

1. **Clean Hands:** The first aider must wash their hands thoroughly before touching any dressing materials.
2. **Clean the wound:**
   - Prepare a solution using 4 to 5 drops of Dettol in a cupful of clear water.
   - Dip sterile gauze into the solution, squeeze off excess liquid, and gently wipe around the wound (not over it) using several pieces of gauze.
   - Pour some of the solution directly over the wound, and lightly clean it from the inside out.
3. **Stop Bleeding:**
   - If bleeding persists, apply pressure with a piece of sterile gauze over the wound for about 10 minutes.
   - Elevate the injured part above the level of the heart to help reduce bleeding.
4. **Dressing:**
   - Once bleeding has stopped, apply Soframycin cream over the wound.
   - Cover the wound with a few layers of sterile gauze.
   - Secure the gauze in place with adhesive plaster or a bandage.

For very minor scratches or cuts:

- Clean the cut with Dettol or soap and water.
- Apply a bandage to cover the wound and keep it protected.

These steps ensure proper cleanliness and treatment for small cuts and scratches to prevent infection and promote healing.

ROAD SAFETY

Some key road safety rules for pedestrians in India:

- **Use Footpaths for Walking:** Always walk on the designated footpaths or sidewalks.
- **Look Both Sides Before Crossing the Road:** Before crossing, look left and right to ensure no vehicles are approaching.
- **Cross the Road through Zebra Crossing:** Use designated pedestrian crossings like zebra crossings where available.
- **Mount and dismount Bus while stationary:** Board or alight from buses only when they are fully stopped.
- **Avoid Foot Board Travel:** Never travel on the footboard of buses or other vehicles.
- **Roads are not playgrounds. Beware:** Children should be supervised and educated about road safety.
- **Never Jump over the Railing:** Avoid crossing over road dividers or barriers.
- **Follow traffic rules, and you will never feel Sorry:** Adhere to traffic signals and regulations for safety.
- **Traffic Warden—Your Partner—to Be Safe on Roads:** Respect and follow guidance from traffic wardens.
- **Avoid Using Mobile Telephones While on the Road:** Focus on the road and surroundings; refrain from distractions like using mobile phones.

These rules help ensure safety for pedestrians and reduce the risk of accidents on the roads.

COMMUNITY SERVICE AND INTEGRATION

THE IMPORTANCE OF COMMUNITY SERVICE AND ITS INTEGRATION INTO SCOUTING AND GUIDING PROGRAMMES

Community service plays a central role in the programs of the Bharat Scouts and Guides (BSG), emphasising the value of contributing to society and improving the lives of others. Through community service, Scouts and Guides learn essential values such as selflessness, teamwork, empathy, and responsibility, all of which align with the core principles of Scouting and Guiding.

The BSG integrates community service into its programs by encouraging Scouts and Guides to participate in activities that benefit local communities, such as cleaning drives, environmental conservation projects, helping the elderly, and supporting the underprivileged. These activities are designed to foster a sense of duty, kindness, and social responsibility, contributing to the development of well-rounded individuals who understand the importance of giving back to society.

Moreover, community service projects in BSG are tied to badges and awards, motivating young people to engage in acts of service. This integration ensures that service becomes a key component of their personal development and is seen as an integral part of their Scouting and Guiding journey.

SCOUTING ACTIVITIES

- **Participate in troop games:** Engage in various games that promote teamwork, physical fitness, and friendly competition within the troop. Games could include relay races, scavenger hunts, or sports like soccer or volleyball.
- **Practice orderly movements and a simple drill for smartness:** Conduct drills that focus on precision and coordination. This could involve marching exercises, flag ceremonies, or learning basic commands to improve discipline and appearance.
- **Participate in two patrol outdoor meetings or a patrol day hike:** Organise outdoor meetings where patrols discuss activities, plan outings, or practice outdoor skills. Alternatively, plan and execute a day hike where patrols navigate a trail, practice orienteering, and practice Leave No Trace principles.

- **Make a gadget or handicraft useful at home:** Encourage scouts to use their creativity and skills to craft useful items. This could range from simple gadgets like bird feeders or plant holders to more complex handicrafts like toolboxes or decorative items.
- **Adopt for the purpose of keeping a park, a water point, a bus stop, or any other public spot or building for a week. Or observe for at least a month the breeding places of mosquitoes and flies and look at their cleanliness:** Take responsibility for maintaining cleanliness and hygiene in a public area like a park, water point, bus stop, or building for a designated period. Alternatively, monitor and report on mosquito breeding sites, promoting awareness and cleanliness efforts.

Participate in any two of the following activities:

I. Discuss with your Scout Master and render some service involving any one of the points of Scout Law, and submit a report to your Scout Master.

Choose a principle from the Scout Law (e.g., helpfulness, obedience) and perform a service project that embodies this principle. Report on the experience and its impact.

II. Undertake a nature study project in consultation with your patrol leader and submit the report within ten days.

Conduct a study on local flora, fauna, or ecological systems. Document findings and present a report highlighting observations and insights gained.

OR

I. Visit a Village Panchayat Samiti, Block Development, Municipality, or Municipal Corporation office and learn about the services rendered by one such public organisation. Submit a report to your Scout Master within ten days.

✓ Visit a local government office (e.g., Panchayat Samiti, Municipality) to learn about their services and responsibilities. Report on their functions, roles in the community, and how they serve the public.

A Patham Sopan Scout/Guide will work for at least six months to qualify for Dwitiya Sopan.

CHAPTER 4

DWITIYA SOPAN

KNOTS AND LASHINGS

TIMBER HITCH

The timber hitch is a knot used to secure a rope to a cylindrical object, such as a log or pole. The knot is known for its ability to hold tight under tension but can be easily untied after the load is removed.

Steps to Tie a Timber Hitch

1. **Position the Rope:** Place the rope around the cylindrical object (e.g., a log or pole). The working end of the rope should be on the side where you want to pull or haul.
2. **Wrap the Working End:** Take the working end of the rope and make a complete turn around the cylindrical object. Ensure that the rope wraps around the object completely.
3. **Add a Second Wrap:** Make another wrap with the working end around the cylindrical object, passing it over the first wrap. This second wrap should be tight and positioned close to the first wrap.
4. **Tuck the Working End:** Pass the working end of the rope under the second wrap you made. This will help to lock the knot in place.
5. **Secure the Knot:** Pull the working end tightly to ensure the wraps are snug around the object. The knot will tighten under load and remain secure.

Uses: The timber hitch is particularly useful for scenarios where you need to haul or lift heavy objects and require a temporary but secure attachment. For instance, you can use this knot to tie

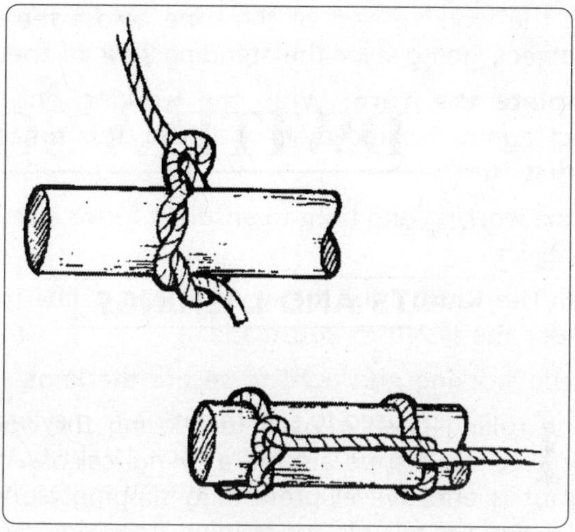

Timber Hitch

a heavy trunk or bundle of bedding, allowing you to drag it to your destination. In camping situations, you can gather collected sticks and logs into bundles and drag them using a piece of string tied with a timber hitch. Its strength and ease of untying, after the load is removed, make it ideal for temporary attachments.

ROLLING HITCH

The rolling hitch is a knot used to attach a rope to a cylindrical object or pole, or to control the direction of a rope under tension.

Steps to Tie a Rolling Hitch

1. **Position the Rope:** Place the rope where you want to secure it around the cylindrical object or pole.
2. **Make the First Turn:** Wrap the working end of the rope around the object, making sure the rope crosses itself on the far side of the object.

Rolling Hitch

Bring the working end of the rope across the near side of the object, going over the standing part of the rope.

3. **Complete the Turn:** Wrap the working end around the object again, making a second turn, this time underneath the first turn.

   Pull the working end tight to ensure it forms a snug fit around the object.

4. **Finish the Knot:** Take the working end of the rope and tuck it under the last turn you made.

   Pull the working end tight to secure the knot.

Uses: The rolling hitch is used for closing the open end of a sack and for securing a rope around a cylindrical object or another rope. This knot is effective in preventing slipping along the object under load, making it reliable for holding items in place.

MARLIN SPIKE or LEVER HITCH

The Marlin Spike Hitch, also known as the Lever Hitch, is a knot used to secure a rope to a cylindrical object, such as a post or a pole. It's known for its ease of use and the leverage it provides for tightening or loosening the rope.

Steps to Tie a Marlin Spike or Lever Hitch

1. **Form a Loop:** Begin by making a loop around the cylindrical object with the rope.
2. **Wrap the Rope:** Take the working end of the rope and wrap it around the cylindrical object in the opposite direction of the loop. Pass it under the standing part of the rope.

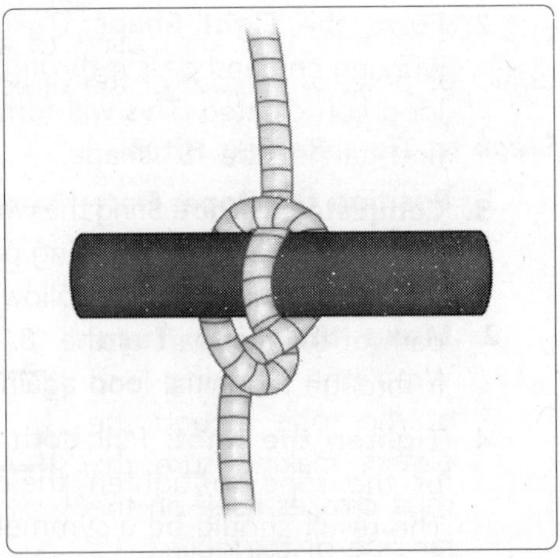

Marlin Spike Hitch

3. **Create a Hitch:** Pull the working end through the loop you formed initially, making sure it lies flat against the cylindrical object.
4. **Tighten the Knot:** Pull the standing part of the rope to tighten the knot. The knot should now be snug around the cylindrical object.

Uses: The Marlin Spike Hitch is used to secure loads on a pole or post, such as when tying down a load on a cart or a vehicle. It's useful for temporary fastening where you may need to quickly release the rope without much effort.

FIGURE OF EIGHT KNOT

The Figure of Eight Knot is a versatile and secure knot commonly used in climbing, sailing, and rescue operations. It is known for its strength and reliability.

Steps to Tie a Figure of Eight Knot

1. **Create a Loop:** Start by making a loop in the rope. Hold the rope in your hand and create a loop by crossing the working end over the standing part of the rope.
2. **Form the Eight Shape:** Take the working end and pass it through the loop you created. This will form the first part of the "8" shape.
3. **Complete the Knot:** Bring the working end back around the standing part of the rope, making sure it follows the path of the first part of the "8." Pass it through the initial loop again.
4. **Tighten the Knot:** Pull both ends of the rope to tighten the knot. The result should be a symmetrical, figure-of-eight shape.

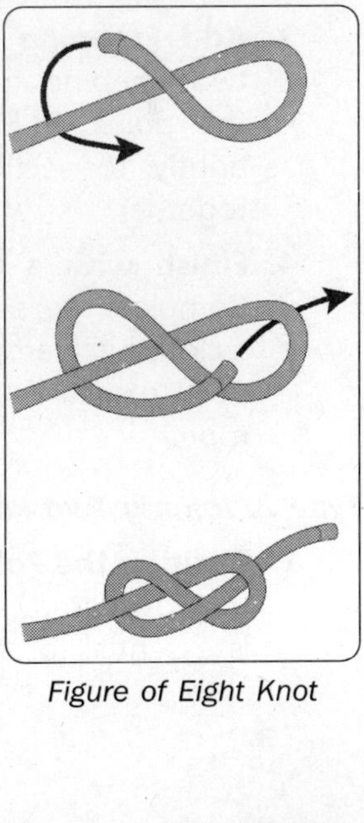

Figure of Eight Knot

Uses: The Figure of Eight Knot is frequently employed as a tie-in knot for climbing harnesses due to its secure and robust nature. It's also used to form a stopper knot at the end of a rope to prevent it from slipping through a block. Additionally, this knot is ideal for securing ropes and harnesses in rescue operations.

SHEER LASHING

Sheer lashing is a technique used in outdoor activities and construction to bind two or more poles or spars together.

Types and Steps

Type 1: Forming Legs from Two Poles

1. **Start with a Clove Hitch:** Begin by tying a clove hitch around one of the poles (not both).

   Twist the free end of the rope around the rope itself to secure it.

2. **Wrap Around the Poles:** Make about ten turns around both poles. Ensure these wraps are not too tight, as this can make it difficult to complete the frapping turns.
3. **Add Frapping Turns:** Make two frapping turns between the poles. Pull these turns tightly to secure the poles together.
4. **Finish with a Clove Hitch:** Complete the lashing by tying a clove hitch around the other pole to secure the end of the rope.

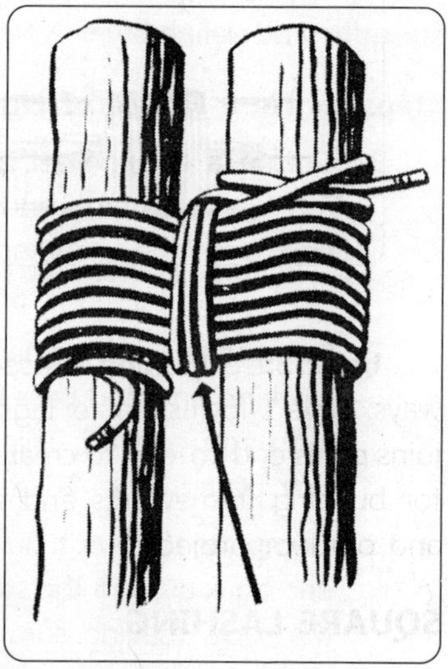

Sheer Lashing

Type 2: Joining Two Poles to Make a Longer Pole

1. **Position the Poles:** Place the two poles side by side, ensuring they overlap by at least a quarter of their lengths. This overlap is essential for creating a stable joint.

2. **Start with a Timber Hitch:** Begin by tying a timber hitch around both poles.
3. **Wrap Around the Poles:** Make about ten turns around both poles. Do not add any frapping turns to this type of lashing.
4. **Finish with a Clove Hitch:** Secure the lashing by tying a clove hitch around one or both poles at the end of the wraps.
5. **Repeat at the other end:** Perform a similar lashing at the other end of the overlap to ensure a firm and secure joint.

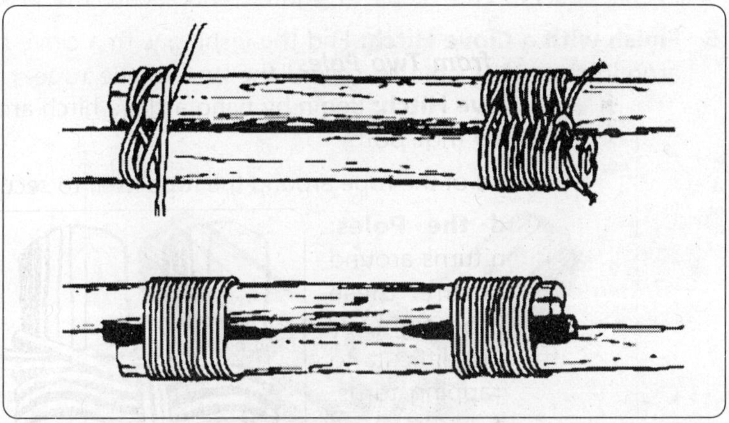

Sheer Lashing

Uses: Sheer lashing is used to secure poles together in two main ways: Type 1 forms stable 'legs' for structures like tripods, while Type 2 joins poles end-to-end to create a longer pole. This technique is valuable for building frameworks and extending reach in various construction and outdoor projects.

SQUARE LASHING

Square lashing is a technique used to join two poles or beams together at a right angle, forming a square or rectangular joint.

Steps

1. **Position the Poles:** Place the two poles at a right angle, ensuring they overlap by at least one-quarter of their lengths.

2. **Start with a Clove Hitch:** Wrap the rope around the top of the vertical pole (or the pole that's being joined) to make a clove hitch. This will secure the start of the lashing.
3. **Wrap around both poles:** Make several tight, even turns around both poles. These wraps should be snug, but not so tight that they become difficult to work with.
4. **Make Frapping Turns:** Create frapping turns by wrapping the rope tightly between the poles, making sure the turns are evenly spaced. This helps to tighten and secure the lashing.
5. **Finish with a Clove Hitch:** End the lashing with a clove hitch around the other pole to secure the end of the rope.

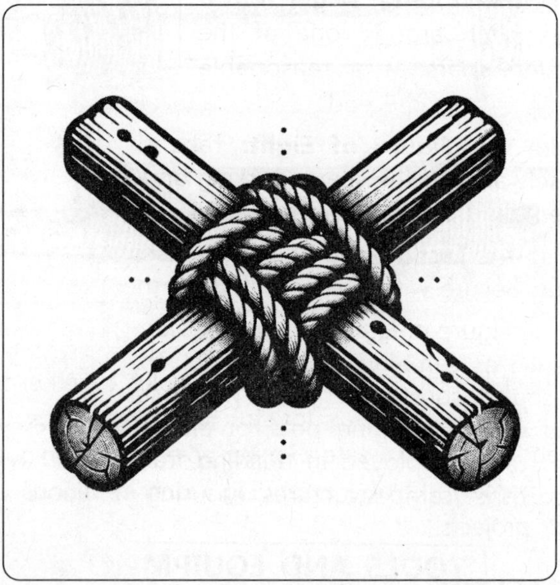

Square Lashing

Uses: Square lashing is essential for constructing stable frameworks, including benches, ladders, and towers. It is particularly useful for creating rectangular or square structures in both outdoor settings and emergency situations. In scouting and camping, it is commonly employed to build functional and durable structures from available materials.

FIGURE OF EIGHT LASHING

The Figure of Eight Lashing is used to lash three poles together to form a tripod, or "gyn." This technique is essential for creating stable structures in various outdoor activities, such as camping and scouting.

Steps

1. **Position the poles:** Lay the three spars (poles) together, ensuring the end of the centre spar points in the opposite direction to the ends of the outer spars.
2. **Start the lashing:** Begin with a clove hitch around one of the outside spars at a reasonable distance from the end.

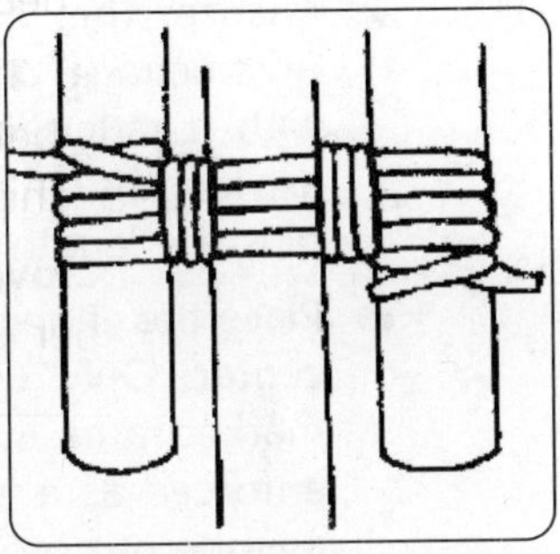

Figure of Eight Lashing

3. **Make the Figure of Eight:** Take six or even turn quite loosely around the spars, working under and over alternately, resembling a figure eight.
4. **Finish the Lashing:** Complete the lashing with loose frapping turns. Secure with a clove hitch on the other outside spar.

Uses: The Figure of Eight Lashing is essential for various outdoor activities, such as camping and scouting. This lashing technique is primarily used to construct tripods, which serve as stable supports for cooking setups, hanging pots, or elevating equipment off the ground. It is also employed in building frameworks for temporary shelters and other camp structures, ensuring stability and reliability.

TOOLS AND EQUIPMENT

HAND AXE or CHOPPER

A hand axe or chopper is a versatile tool essential for various tasks in outdoor activities like camping and woodcraft. When chopping and splitting wood, it's crucial to have a sturdy wood support underneath, such as a downed tree or a large chunk of wood, to prevent the axe from striking the ground and losing its effectiveness.

Using a Hand Axe

1. **Chopping Area Preparation:**
   - Designate a clear chopping area near the fire but separate from it by a graded woodpile.
   - Ensure the area is free of obstructions and trip hazards, with a radius of at least three axe lengths (an outstretched arm plus the length of three axes).
   - Place the chopping block in the center. Only use axes in this marked area, which should be enforced as a 'no-go' zone for anyone not properly trained or clothed.

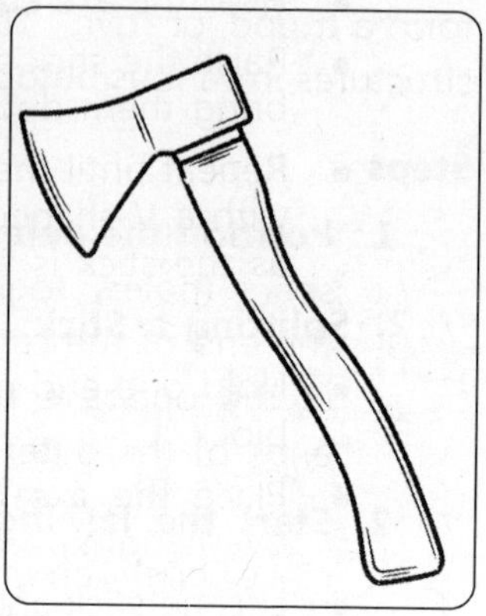

Hand Axe

2. **Chopping Position:**
   - Crouch or kneel behind the chopping block.
   - Hold the wood to be chopped in one hand and grip the axe haft firmly with the other.
3. **Aiming and Chopping:**
   - Aim carefully, trying to hit the same spot on the wood each time. Using a chalk mark on the log can help when practicing.
   - Swing the axe in a chopping motion by bending your arm at the elbow. Aim to create a small 'V' with alternate angled cuts at 45 degrees. Avoid chopping straight down to prevent the axe head from bouncing.
4. **Splitting the wood:**
   - As the 'V' widens, it will create chippings, and the wood will soon split. Regularly clear away chippings and use them for kindling.
   - Ensure the wood is supported by a sturdy surface, such as a downed tree or large chunk of wood, to prevent the axe stroke from hitting the ground.

Chopping and Splitting Techniques

1. **Chopping a Stick in Two:**
   - Hold the axe edge against the stick at a slant to the grain.
   - Raise the stick and axe together with a wrist motion, then bring them down hard on the chopping block.
   - Repeat until the stick is cut. If the stick is too thick, cut it with a V-shaped notch, making the top of the V as wide as the stick is thick.
2. **Splitting a Stick:**
   - Hold one end of the stick, and rest the other end on the block.
   - Place the axe blade on the stick's end, with a portion overhanging.
   - Lift the stick and axe together and bring them down hard on the chopping block. Twist the wood or axe slightly on impact to break the pieces apart.
3. **Splitting thick wood:**
   - For wrist-thick or thicker wood, saw it into pieces about the length of your axe handle.
   - Split the halves into quarters, and the quarters into eighths.

DAGGER AND SCOUT KNIFE

A dagger is a pointed, double-edged knife designed primarily for thrusting or stabbing, often used in close combat and self-defence, featuring a sharp point and typically a guard to protect the hand. In contrast, a scout knife is a versatile, multi-purpose tool designed for scouts and outdoor enthusiasts, featuring a folding blade and additional tools like screwdrivers and can openers, making it compact, portable, and ideal for various outdoor tasks and activities.

Dagger

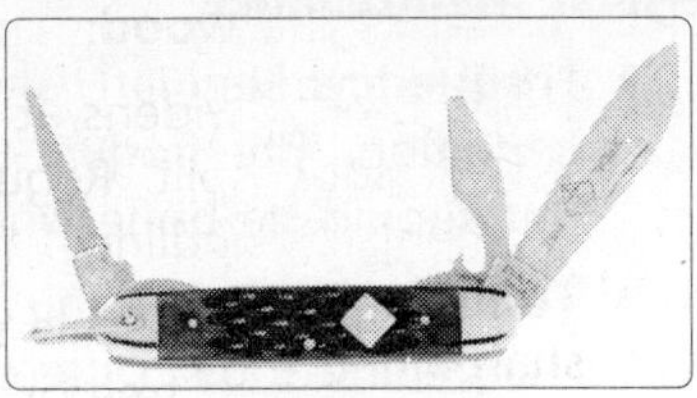

Scout Knife

Opening the Knife

- **Grip:** Hold the knife in your left hand, ensuring your fingers are clear of the blade's path.
- **Opening Action:** Insert your right thumbnail into the nail slot on the blade. Pull the blade out until it clicks into the open position. Ensure the blade locks securely before use.

Closing the Knife

- **Grip:** Hold the knife handle firmly with your left hand, keeping your fingers clear of the blade.
- **Closing Action:** Push against the back of the blade with your right hand's fingers to release the lock. Allow the blade to snap shut gently. Avoid forcing the blade to prevent damage.

Safety

- **Cut Away from Yourself:** Always direct the blade away from your body and hands to prevent accidental cuts.
- **Finger Placement:** Keep your fingers and hands clear of the cutting path. Use your thumb and fingers to guide the blade rather than placing your hands near the cutting area.
- **Stable Surface:** Ensure you are working on a stable surface to maintain control. A wobbly or unstable surface can lead to accidents.
- **Proper Handling:** Fully open the knife before use and ensure it is securely closed when not in use to avoid unintentional injuries.
- **Storage:** Store the knife in a safe place, preferably in a sheath or protective cover, to prevent accidental injuries and damage.

Regular Maintenance

- **Frequency:** Regularly sharpen your knife to keep it in optimal condition. The frequency of sharpening depends on usage but should be done whenever the blade starts to feel dull.
- **Tools:** Use a sharpening stone, honing rod, or other appropriate sharpening tools. Different tools may be required for specific types of blades.

Sharpening Technique

- **Consistent Angle:** Maintain a consistent sharpening angle to ensure an even edge. Typically, this angle is around 20 degrees for most knives. This consistency is key to achieving a sharp and durable edge.
- **Motion:** Use a smooth, steady motion across the sharpening surface. Follow the natural curve of the blade to achieve a uniform sharpness.
- **Check the Edge:** Regularly check the edge for sharpness and make sure there are no nicks or irregularities.

Cleaning and Protection

- **After Sharpening:** Clean the blade to remove any metal filings or residue left from sharpening.
- **Oil Application:** Apply a thin layer of oil to the blade to prevent rust and corrosion. This is particularly important if the knife is made of carbon steel or if it is exposed to moisture.
- **Storage:** Store the knife in a dry, cool place to maintain its condition and sharpness.

Uses

1. **Coarse Cutting:**
    - **Grasping:** For tasks like trimming branches or cutting through tougher materials, hold the handle firmly with your whole hand. This grip gives you better control and power.
    - **Cutting Technique:** Cut away from your body to minimise the risk of injury. Work from the thick end of the material towards the thinner end, using a sawing motion if necessary. This approach helps manage thicker material and provides a cleaner cut.
2. **Fine Whittling:**
    - **Short Cuts:** When performing detailed work, such as carving or whittling, use short, deliberate cuts. These cuts help in controlling the shape and precision of the material being worked on.
    - **Pushing Technique:** For more control, push the back of the blade with your thumb. This technique allows for finer and more accurate cuts, especially for intricate details.

SCREWDRIVER

A screwdriver is a hand tool used for driving screws into materials by turning the screw head. It typically features a handle and a shaft with a tip designed to fit specific screw types, such as flathead or Phillips. Screwdrivers can be manual or powered, making them essential for various construction and repair tasks.

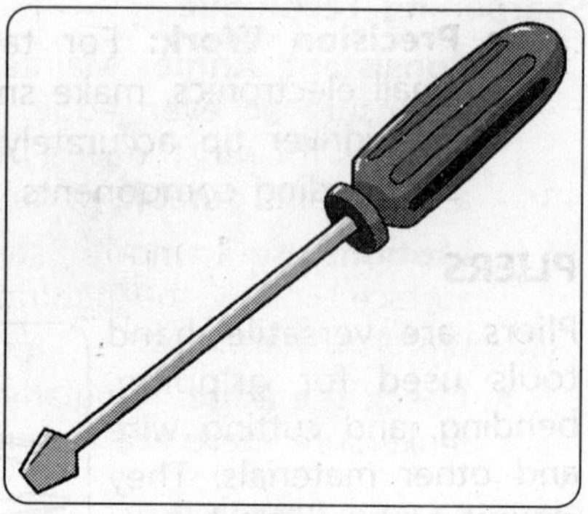

Screwdriver

Uses

- **Driving Screws:** Screwdrivers are essential for inserting and removing screws in various materials. Match the screwdriver type (e.g., flathead, Phillips, or Torx) to the screw head to ensure a proper fit and avoid stripping the screw.
- **Adjusting Components:** Useful for fine adjustments, such as adjusting electronic components, opening battery compartments, or assembling or disassembling items like furniture or appliances.

Safety

- **Correct Type:** Always select the right screwdriver type and size for the job. A mismatched screwdriver can damage the screw or tool and lead to slippage, causing injury.
- **Handle Grip:** Use the handle for a firm grip. Avoid applying excessive force, as it can cause the screwdriver to slip, potentially injuring your hand or damaging the workpiece.
- **Inspection:** Before use, check the screwdriver for any damage, including cracks in the handle or wear on the tip. A damaged screwdriver may not function correctly and can be unsafe.

Technique

- **Driving Screws:** Insert the screwdriver tip into the screw head. Turn the handle clockwise to drive the screw into the material or anticlockwise to remove it. Apply steady, controlled pressure to avoid stripping the screw.

- **Precision Work:** For tasks requiring precision, such as small electronics, make small, controlled turns and align the screwdriver tip accurately to avoid slipping and damaging surrounding components.

PLIERS

Pliers are versatile hand tools used for gripping, bending, and cutting wire and other materials. They consist of two metal arms joined at a pivot point, with jaws at one end and handles at the other. Pliers come in various types, including needle-nose, slip-joint, and cutting pliers, each suited for specific tasks.

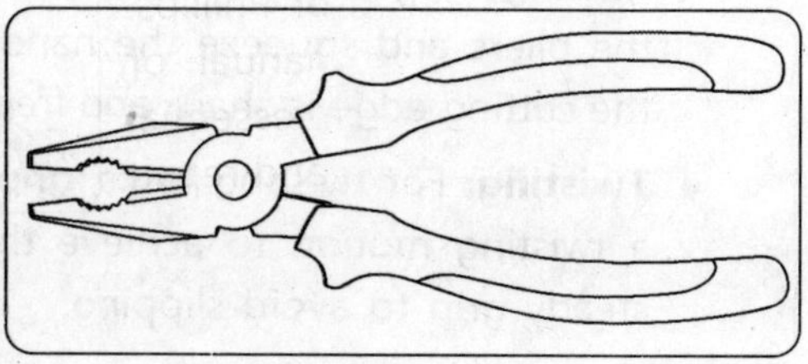

Pliers

Uses

- **Gripping and Holding:** Pliers are versatile tools for gripping, holding, and manipulating objects. They are particularly useful for bending wire, holding small parts, or gripping nuts and bolts.
- **Cutting:** Certain pliers, like side cutters or wire cutters, can cut through wire or other materials. This function is useful for tasks like trimming excess wire or cutting small components.
- **Twisting and Turning:** Needle-nose pliers are ideal for twisting or turning small components, making them useful in detailed work or reaching into tight spaces.

Safety

- **Correct Type:** Use the appropriate type of pliers for the task. For example, use needle-nose pliers for precision work and locking pliers for firm gripping. Using the wrong type can result in inefficient work or tool damage.
- **Handle Grip:** Hold the pliers by the handles and avoid pinching your fingers or hands. Ensure your grip is firm but not excessive to maintain control and avoid slipping.
- **Inspection:** Regularly check for signs of wear or damage, such as loose or misaligned jaws, which could affect performance and safety.

Technique

- **Gripping:** Position the object between the jaws of the pliers and squeeze the handles to grip it firmly. Ensure that the jaws are aligned properly to avoid damaging the object.
- **Cutting:** Align the wire or material with the cutting edge of the pliers and squeeze the handles to cut through it. Ensure the cutting edge is sharp and free from damage for clean cuts.
- **Twisting:** For twisting tasks, grip the object securely and use a twisting motion to achieve the desired result. Maintain a steady grip to avoid slipping.

HAMMER

A hammer is a tool used for striking objects, driving nails, and breaking materials. It typically consists of a heavy metal head attached to a long handle, providing leverage and force. Hammers come in various types, such as claw hammers for pulling nails, sledgehammers for heavy-duty tasks, and ball-peen hammers for metalworking.

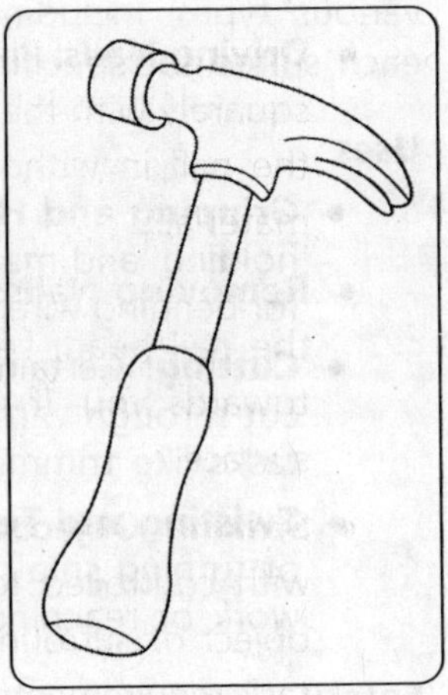

Hammer

Uses

- **Driving Nails:** Hammers are commonly used to drive nails into materials such as wood. This is essential for construction, carpentry, and various repair tasks.
- **Removing Nails:** The claw end of the hammer can be used to pull nails out. This is useful for disassembling items or correcting mistakes.
- **General Striking:** Hammers are also used for other tasks like breaking objects, fitting parts together, or shaping metal, making them versatile tools in various applications.

Safety

- **Proper Grip:** Hold the hammer by the handle, wrapping your fingers around it and keeping your thumb on the opposite side for a secure grip. This ensures better control and reduces the risk of injury.
- **Target Area:** Ensure that the area where you are working is clear of obstructions and that you have a stable surface. Avoid striking your hand or fingers accidentally.
- **Inspection:** Regularly inspect the hammer for damage, such as a loose or cracked handle. A damaged hammer can be dangerous and less effective.

Technique

- **Driving Nails:** Place the nail in the desired location and strike it squarely with the hammerhead. Use controlled swings to drive the nail in without bending it or damaging the surrounding material.
- **Removing Nails:** Position the claw end of the hammer under the nail head. Lever the nail out by pulling the handle back towards you. If needed, use a block of wood to protect the surface.
- **Striking Objects:** Use the hammerhead to strike the object with controlled force. Ensure accuracy to avoid damaging the object or surrounding area, and adjust the force based on the task requirements.

SAFETY RULES FOR USING HAND TOOLS

1. **Inspect Tools Before Use:** Check hand tools for any signs of damage or wear before use. Ensure handles are secure, blades are sharp, and there are no cracks or defects.
2. **Use the Right Tool for the Job:** Always select the appropriate tool for the task at hand. Using the wrong tool can lead to injury or damage to the tool or workpiece.

3. **Keep Tools in Good Condition:** Regularly maintain and sharpen tools to ensure they function properly. Replace or repair damaged tools promptly.
4. **Use Tools Correctly:** Follow the manufacturer's instructions for proper use. For example, use screwdrivers with the correct type and size for the screws, and use hammers to drive nails without excessive force.
5. **Secure the Workpiece:** Ensure the material you are working on is securely clamped or held in place. This prevents the workpiece from shifting and reduces the risk of accidents.
6. **Maintain a Safe Working Environment:** Work in a clean, well-lit area with adequate space. Remove any obstacles or hazards that could cause accidents or interfere with your work.
7. **Use Tools with Both Hands When Necessary:** For tasks that require greater control or force, use both hands to handle the tool. This provides better stability and reduces the risk of slipping.
8. **Store Tools Properly:** When not in use, store tools in a designated place, such as a toolbox or tool rack. Keep sharp edges and blades covered to prevent accidental injuries.
9. **Wear appropriate safety gear:** Depending on the task, wear safety goggles, gloves, or other protective equipment to safeguard against debris, sharp edges, or other hazards.
10. **Avoid Distractions:** Focus on the task at hand and avoid distractions that could lead to mishandling of tools or accidents.
11. **Handle Tools with Care:** Avoid using excessive force, and never use tools for purposes they are not designed for. For instance, do not use a wrench as a hammer or a screwdriver as a pry bar.
12. **Pass Tools Safely:** When handing tools to someone, pass them handle-first to prevent accidents and ensure the recipient has a secure grip.

FIRECRAFT

CAMPFIRE

A campfire is primarily used for general warmth, cooking, and providing light, creating a cosy gathering spot for campers.

Log Cabin Fire

- **Setup:** Arrange logs in a square or rectangular shape with a small gap in the centre for kindling and tinder.
- **Building:** Start with a layer of kindling and tinder in the center. Place the first layer of logs around the kindling, then add additional layers of logs in a criss-cross pattern to form a stable, self-supporting structure.

Log Cabin Fire

- **Advantages:** It provides a stable base, is easy to maintain, and is good for extended use.

Teepee Fire

- **Setup:** Stack kindling and small logs in a conical shape, with a space in the centre for air and ignition.
- **Building:** Place tinder in the centre and arrange kindling around it, then add progressively larger logs.
- **Advantages:** It burns quickly and efficiently, making it good for immediate warmth and cooking.

Teepee Fire

COOKING FIRE

The cooking fire is specifically designed to prepare meals, utilising methods like the Star Fire or Dutch Oven Fire to facilitate efficient and effective cooking.

Star Fire

- **Setup:** Lay logs out in a star pattern with the tips of the logs pointing outward and the centre open.
- **Building:** Place kindling and tinder in the center. As the fire grows, you can place pots and pans around the central fire.
- **Advantages:** Allows for multiple cooking areas around the fire, making it good for cooking meals for larger groups.

Star Fire

Dutch Oven Fire

- **Setup:** Build a bed of hot coals or embers in a circular pattern.
- **Building:** Place a Dutch oven directly on top of the coals or use a rack to elevate it slightly. The lid can also be covered with hot coals for even cooking.
- **Advantages:** Provides consistent, even heat for slow cooking, ideal for baking and stewing.

Dutch Oven Fire

SIGNAL FIRE

A signal fire is crucial in emergency situations or for marking locations, as it produces significant smoke or a large flame visible from a distance, which can attract attention and aid in rescue efforts.

- **Setup:** Build a large fire with a noticeable amount of smoke.
- **Building:** Use a mix of dry and green materials. Adding green leaves or branches will increase the smoke output.

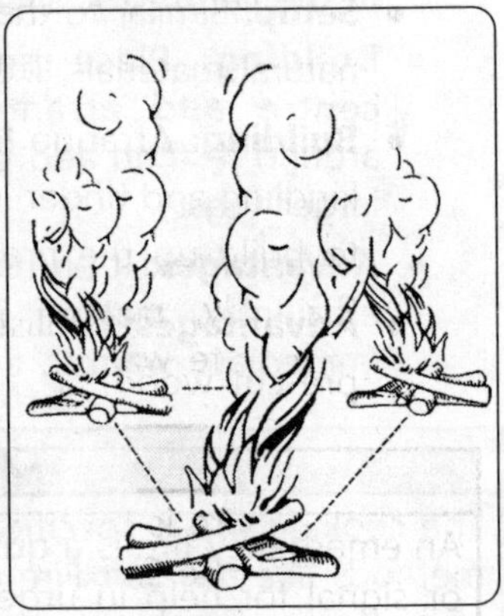

Signal Fire

- **Advantages:** High visibility for signalling over long distances, important for emergency situations.

SURVIVAL FIRE

The survival fire is essential for warmth and boiling water in critical situations, requiring a well-constructed fire lay to ensure it is reliable and easy to maintain.

Fire Lay

- **Setup:** Start with a small pile of tinder, followed by thin, small pieces of wood, and then larger logs.
- **Building:** Arrange materials to form a small, manageable fire. Use a log cabin or teepee style to keep the fire focused and efficient.
- **Advantages:** Quick to build and maintain, provides essential heat and allows for water boiling.

BACKWOODS FIRE

The backwoods fire is used in more remote settings, relying on natural materials and traditional techniques to create a sustainable fire.

Log Cabin Backwoods Fire

- **Setup:** Similar to the log cabin fire but adapted to use available natural materials like branches and small logs.
- **Building:** Arrange logs in a square or rectangular shape with kindling and tinder in the center. Use the surrounding materials to build up the fire.
- **Advantages:** Utilises local resources, less dependence on pre-cut wood.

EMERGENCY FIRE

An emergency fire is a quick and effective method to produce heat or signal for help in urgent situations.

Fire Triangle

- **Setup:** Arrange materials in a triangular shape with dry tinder in the centre.
- **Building:** Start with a small pile of tinder, then add kindling in a triangular shape. Build up the fire as needed.
- **Advantages:** Quick to set up, ideal for emergencies where speed is essential.

LAYING AND LIGHTING A WOOD FIRE IN THE OPEN WITH NOT MORE THAN TWO MATCHSTICKS

Creating a wood fire with just two matchsticks requires careful preparation and technique. Here's how to do it:

Preparation

1. **Select a Safe Site:**
    - Choose a clear, flat area free of flammable materials like leaves or dry grass. Ensure it's away from overhanging branches and other hazards.
2. **Gather Materials:**
    - **Tinder:** Small, highly flammable materials such as dry leaves, grass, pine needles, or thin bark.
    - **Kindling:** Small sticks or twigs, slightly larger than the tinder, that catch fire from the tinder.
    - **Fuel Wood:** Larger logs or branches that will sustain the fire once the kindling is burning.
3. **Prepare the Fire Lay:**
    - **Tinder Nest:** Form a small nest of tinder in the centre of your fire area.
    - **Kindling Setup:** Arrange the kindling over the tinder in a teepee or crisscross pattern, leaving gaps for air to circulate.
    - **Fuel Wood Arrangement:** Place the larger fuel wood around the kindling, forming a loose teepee or log cabin structure to support the kindling.

Lighting the Fire

1. **Ensure Dryness:** Make sure all materials are dry. Wet or damp materials can be difficult to ignite and may hinder the fire.
2. **Use the First Matchstick:**
   - **Strike the Match:** Hold the matchstick away from your body. Strike it against the matchbox or striking surface, making sure to shield the flame from the wind.
   - **Ignite the Tinder:** Carefully hold the lit matchstick to the tinder nest. Let the flame catch the tinder.
3. **Encourage the Flame:**
   - **Blow Gently:** Once the tinder begins to burn, gently blow on it to help the flames spread to the kindling.
   - **Add Kindling:** As the tinder burns, add small pieces of kindling, ensuring not to smother the flame.
4. **Use the Second Matchstick (if needed):** If the first matchstick fails or the tinder does not catch, use the second matchstick to try again. Adjust the materials if necessary to improve ignition.
5. **Add Fuel Wood:** As the kindling starts burning well, gradually add larger pieces of fuel wood to sustain the fire. Arrange them to allow proper airflow.
6. **Monitor the Fire:** Keep an eye on the fire to ensure it remains contained and burns steadily. Adjust the wood as needed to maintain a good flame.

FIRE PRECAUTIONS

- **Selection of a Fire Site:** When selecting a site for building a fire, choose an area that is safe and free from potential hazards. The site should be located away from flammable materials, such as dry leaves, branches, and other combustibles. Avoid placing the fire near structures, tents, or overhanging branches that could catch fire. Ensure that the site is well-ventilated and that there is sufficient clearance around the area to prevent the accidental spreading of flames. By carefully selecting a suitable location, you minimise the risk of accidental fires and ensure a safer environment for all.

- **Fire Construction:** Constructing a fire properly is essential for safety and effectiveness. Use fire pits or designated fire zones to contain the fire and prevent it from spreading. The construction should involve arranging fuel in a controlled manner, typically using a teepee or log cabin structure to allow for proper airflow and ignition. Avoid making the fire too large; instead, build it to a manageable size appropriate for the task. By keeping the fire contained and appropriately sized, you reduce the risk of uncontrolled spread and enhance the safety of the fire.
- **Fuel Management:** Proper fuel management is crucial for maintaining fire safety. Use dry, seasoned wood or other suitable fuels to ensure a clean and manageable burn. Avoid using flammable liquids, such as gasoline or alcohol, to ignite or sustain the fire, as these can lead to dangerous flare-ups and uncontrollable fires. Store fuel away from the fire site in a safe location where it will not be accidentally ignited. By managing fuel carefully and using only approved materials, you contribute to a safer and more controlled fire environment.
- **Fire Lighting:** When lighting a fire, use safe and approved methods to minimise the risk of accidents. If you need to light a fire with limited matches, adopt a methodical approach: construct a small, easily ignitable fire structure, such as a tinder bundle, and light it with precision. Avoid using excessive matches or lighters, which can lead to mishandling and increased risk. By following safe lighting practices, you ensure a controlled ignition and reduce the potential for accidental fires.
- **Supervision:** Constant supervision of the fire is essential for maintaining safety. Never leave the fire unattended, as this can lead to accidental spreading or uncontrolled flames. Designate a responsible person to monitor the fire at all times, ensuring that it remains contained and manageable. Establish a system for checking the fire regularly and addressing any issues that arise. By keeping a watchful eye

on the fire, you can prevent potential hazards and ensure a safer environment for everyone involved.

- **Extinguishing the Fire:** Properly extinguishing a fire is critical to preventing it from reigniting. When finished with the fire, use water or dirt to thoroughly douse the flames, ensuring that the fire is completely out. Stir the ashes to check for any remaining embers, and continue adding water or dirt until the ashes are cold to the touch. Verify that the fire site is fully extinguished before leaving the area. This thorough approach helps prevent accidental fires and ensures that the site is safe for others.
- **Clothing and Safety:** Wearing appropriate clothing and safety gear is important when working with or near a fire. Avoid loose or flammable clothing that could catch fire. Opt for fire-resistant or protective clothing when handling fire-related tasks. Keep a fire extinguisher, bucket of water, or other fire suppression equipment nearby to quickly address any emergencies. By dressing safely and having proper equipment on hand, you reduce the risk of personal injury and enhance overall fire safety.
- **Emergency Procedures:** Being prepared for emergencies is essential to fire safety. Familiarise yourself with fire safety procedures and ensure that all members know how to respond in case of an uncontrolled fire. Establish emergency contacts and a plan for alerting authorities if needed. Conduct regular fire drills to practice emergency responses and ensure everyone knows their role. By having a clear understanding of emergency procedures, you can effectively manage fire situations and ensure the safety of all participants.
- **Training and Awareness:** Proper training and awareness are key components of fire safety. Ensure that all Scouts and Guides receive training in fire safety practices, including the proper use of fire equipment and emergency response procedures. Conduct regular safety briefings and fire drills to reinforce knowledge and preparedness. By investing in training and maintaining awareness, you help ensure that all participants are equipped to handle fire-related situations safely and effectively.

EXTINGUISHING METHODS

BUCKET CHAIN METHOD

The bucket chain method is a traditional and effective technique for extinguishing fires, especially in scenarios where modern firefighting equipment is unavailable. This method relies on the coordinated efforts of a group of people to transport water from a source to the fire site, providing a continuous flow of water to douse the flames.

Step-by-Step Procedure:

1. **Form a Line:** Organise a line of people extending from the water source (such as a well, river, or tank) to the fire. Each person in the line will be responsible for passing buckets of water from one person to the next.
2. **Fill Buckets:** The person closest to the water source fills a bucket with water.
3. **Pass Buckets:** The filled bucket is handed to the next person in the line. This process continues down the line until the bucket reaches the person closest to the fire.
4. **Empty Buckets:** The person at the end of the line pours the water onto the fire. Once emptied, the bucket is sent back along the line to the water source.
5. **Repeat:** This process is repeated continuously, creating a steady stream of water being transported from the source to the fire.

Advantages of the Bucket Chain Method

Accessibility

- **Minimal Equipment Required:** The method requires only basic items like buckets and a water source, making it accessible in virtually any environment. There is no need for specialised firefighting tools or vehicles.
- **No Technical Skills Needed:** Participants do not need extensive training or technical skills to be effective. Simple instructions on forming the line and passing buckets are sufficient, allowing even untrained individuals to contribute effectively.

Simplicity

- **Easy to Implement:** The process is straightforward and can be quickly organized. In emergencies, simplicity is crucial, as it allows for rapid deployment without the need for complex planning.
- **Effective Communication:** Clear, simple communication can be maintained among participants, ensuring that everyone knows their role and can act cohesively.

Community Effort

- **Engages the Local Community:** The method fosters a sense of community and collective responsibility. It encourages local residents to work together, which can strengthen community bonds and ensure a rapid response to emergencies.
- **Shared Responsibility:** Involving multiple people distributes the workload, preventing any single individual from becoming overwhelmed. This shared responsibility can also lead to better morale and cooperation.

Cost-Effective

- **Low Cost:** Buckets and simple protective gear are inexpensive compared to advanced firefighting equipment. This makes the method affordable for communities with limited financial resources.
- **No Maintenance:** Unlike mechanical equipment, buckets do not require maintenance or repairs, reducing long-term costs.

Tackling Dry Grass Fire

Dry grass fires can spread rapidly and pose significant risks to life and property. Effective methods and strategies are essential to controlling and extinguishing these fires. Some ways to take care of it are as follows:

1. **Creating a Fire Belt:** Creating a fire belt involves chopping down grass and plants around the fire to prevent it from spreading. This technique starves the fire of fuel, effectively containing it within a designated area.

- **Identify the Fire's Path:** Assess the direction in which the fire is spreading.
- **Clear Vegetation:** Using tools such as machetes, axes, or even shovels, clear the grass and plants around the fire, creating a barrier.
- **Width of the Fire Belt:** Ensure the fire belt is wide enough to prevent the fire from jumping over. Typically, a width of several metres is recommended, depending on the fire's intensity and wind conditions.

2. **Throwing Sand, Soil, and Water:** Utilise available resources such as sand, soil, and water to extinguish the fire. Throw these materials with force directly onto the flames.

   Using Sand and Soil:

   - **Shovels or Buckets:** Use shovels or buckets to throw sand or soil onto the fire. This helps smother the flames and cut off their oxygen supply.
   - **Covering the Fire:** Ensure the sand or soil completely covers the flames to effectively suffocate them.

   Using Water:

   - **Direct Application:** If water is available, throw it directly onto the flames. Aim for the base of the fire, where it is most effective.
   - **Continuous Supply:** Ensure a continuous supply of water to maintain the firefighting effort until the fire is completely extinguished.

Effectively tackling a dry grass fire involves a combination of creating fire belts, using available resources like sand, soil, and water, and employing the bucket chain method for efficient material transport. Prioritising safety and maintaining clear communication with your team are essential for successfully managing and extinguishing the fire. By following the above mentioned steps and techniques, one can effectively control and extinguish dry grass fires, protecting both life and property.

COOKING

WORKING AND MAINTENANCE OF A KEROSENE STOVE, PRESSURE STOVE, AND GAS STOVE

KEROSENE STOVE

A wick kerosene stove is a cooking device that uses cotton wicks to absorb and burn kerosene for heat. It consists of a fuel tank for storage, cotton wicks to draw fuel, a burner for combustion, a flame regulator knob to control heat, a chimney (optional) for airflow, and a metal body to support cookware.

Working

- **Fuel Absorption :** Cotton wicks absorb kerosene from the tank through capillary action, ensuring a continuous fuel supply.
- **Ignition :** The top of the wicks is lit, vaporising kerosene and creating a stable flame for cooking.
- **Combustion :** The fuel burns steadily, generating consistent heat suitable for various cooking needs.
- **Heat Transfer :** The metal surface of the stove conducts and distributes heat to the cooking vessel efficiently.

Maintenance:

- **Clean the Wicks :** Trim burnt ends regularly or replace old wicks to maintain a steady and smokeless flame.
- **Clean the Burner :** Remove carbon deposits by soaking the burner in warm water and scrubbing with a brush.
- **Regular Cleaning :** Rinse the tank occasionally with clean kerosene to prevent fuel contamination.
- **Ensure Ventilation :** Use the stove in an open area to avoid smoke buildup and carbon monoxide poisoning.

PRESSURE STOVE

A pressure stove is a type of stove that uses liquid fuel, typically kerosene or other similar fuels, which is pressurised before being vaporised and ignited at the burner. The stove requires manual pressurisation of the fuel tank by pumping air into it. This pressure forces the fuel through a jet, where it is vaporised and then ignited to produce a hot, efficient flame. Pressure stoves are often used for outdoor activities, camping, and emergency situations due to their high heat output and efficiency.

Working

- **Fuel Filling:** Fill the fuel tank with the appropriate fuel, typically kerosene, ensuring it is not overfilled.
- **Pressurising:** Pump air into the fuel tank using the built-in pump to create the necessary pressure. This pressure forces the fuel through the stove.
- **Priming and Lighting:** Preheat the burner by allowing a small amount of fuel to vaporise and ignite it. Once the burner is hot, open the main valve to allow a steady flow of vaporised fuel to the burner and light it.
- **Cooking:** Adjust the flame using the control valve. Place your cooking vessel on the burner and cook as needed.

Maintenance

- **Pump and Valve Inspection:** Regularly check and maintain the pump and valves. Lubricate and replace washers and seals as necessary to ensure efficient operation.
- **Burner Cleaning:** Clean the burner to remove soot and carbon deposits that can affect performance.
- **Check for Leaks:** Inspect the stove for fuel leaks, particularly at connections and joints. Replace any worn or damaged parts promptly.
- **Use Quality Fuel:** Use clean, high-quality fuel to prevent clogging and ensure efficient operation.

GAS STOVE

A gas stove is a cooking appliance that uses combustible gas, such as propane, butane, or natural gas, as a fuel source. It features burners connected to a gas supply via a regulator and control valves. When the gas is ignited, it produces a flame that can be adjusted for various cooking purposes. Gas stoves are widely used in both household kitchens and outdoor settings due to their convenience, ease of use, and precise temperature control.

Working

- **Connecting the Cylinder:** Ensure the gas cylinder is securely connected to the stove. Check for proper fitting to avoid leaks.
- **Lighting:** Turn the control knob to the ignition position and ignite the burner using a lighter or the stove's built-in igniter.
- **Flame Adjustment:** Adjust the control knob to regulate the flame intensity for cooking.
- **Cooking:** Place your cooking vessel on the burner and adjust the flame as needed for your cooking requirements.

Maintenance

- **Regular Cleaning:** Clean the burners, grates, and surfaces regularly to remove food spills and grease buildup.
- **Check for Gas Leaks:** Periodically check the gas connections for leaks using a soap solution. If bubbles form, there is a leak that needs fixing.
- **Burner Maintenance:** Remove and clean the burners to ensure they are free of debris and functioning efficiently.
- **Valve and Regulator Check:** Inspect the gas valves and regulators for proper functioning. Replace any faulty components immediately.
- **Hose Inspection:** Regularly check the gas hose for any signs of wear or damage. Replace it if necessary to prevent leaks.

COOKING IN THE OPEN

Cooking in the open is an essential skill for Scouts and Guides, especially during camping and outdoor activities. Following proper guidelines ensures safety and efficiency while preparing meals.

1. **Preparing the Cooking Area**
   - **Selection of Site:** Choose a safe and level area for cooking that is away from flammable materials, such as dry grass, leaves, or overhanging branches. Ensure the area is well-ventilated and free from strong winds that could affect the fire or stove operation.
   - **Clearance:** Clear the area of debris and ensure there is sufficient space around the cooking area to avoid accidents. Keep a safe distance from tents and other camp structures.
2. **Setting Up the Fire or Stove**
   - **Fire Safety:** When using an open fire, dig a small pit or use a fire ring to contain the flames. Surround the pit with a circle of stones to prevent the fire from spreading. Never leave the fire unattended.
   - **Using Stoves:** For kerosene or pressure stoves, place them on a stable, non-flammable surface. Ensure the stove is set up according to the manufacturer's instructions. For gas stoves, ensure the connection is secure and the stove is placed on a flat, stable surface.
3. **Fuel Management**
   - **Wood for Fires:** Use dry, seasoned wood for fuel. Avoid using green or wet wood, as it produces excessive smoke and is harder to burn.
   - **Fuel for Stoves:** Store fuel safely, away from the cooking area, and handle it with care to avoid spills. Ensure that the fuel container is securely closed and labelled.
4. **Lighting the Fire or Stove**
   - **Fire Lighting:** Use safe methods to light a fire, such as using matches or a lighter. Avoid using flammable liquids to ignite the fire, as this can be dangerous. Ensure the fire is fully established before starting to cook.

- **Stove Ignition:** Follow the manufacturer's instructions for lighting the stove. For kerosene and pressure stoves, ensure proper priming and pressurisation before ignition.

5. Cooking Practices

- **Safe Cooking:** Always use appropriate cooking utensils and ensure they are clean. Never leave cooking unattended, and use heat-resistant gloves or pot holders when handling hot cookware.
- **Temperature Control:** Adjust the flame or heat source to control the cooking temperature. Use a lid or cover to maintain heat and speed up cooking.

6. Post-Cooking Procedures

- **Extinguishing Fires:** After you finish cooking, it's essential to completely extinguish the fire to ensure safety. Start by letting the fire burn down as much as possible. Once it has, scatter the coals, break up any large pieces, and separate logs. Stir the coals and sprinkle them with water, continuing to stir until no live embers remain, even in the centre or under the logs. If water isn't available, use sand or dirt to cover the coals and stir thoroughly. Make sure the area is cool to the touch before leaving, and cover it with rocks or additional dirt. Always double-check to ensure the fire is completely out before departing.
- **Cleaning Up:** Clean the cooking area and utensils thoroughly. Dispose of food scraps and trash in designated waste containers, or pack them out. Leave the cooking site clean and as you found it.

7. Safety Measures

- **Fire Extinguishing:** Keep a fire extinguisher, water bucket, or sand available at the cooking site for emergency use.
- **Clothing:** Wear appropriate clothing that is resistant to heat and flame. Tuck loose ends of clothing to prevent them from catching fire.
- **First Aid:** Have a basic first aid kit on hand and be aware of how to treat minor burns or injuries.

SAFETY PRECAUTIONS IN CASE OF A GAS LEAK

Gas leaks can pose serious risks, including fire and health hazards. Following these safety precautions is crucial for preventing accidents and ensuring safety in case of a gas leak during scouting and guiding activities.

1. **Immediate Response**
   - **Smell of Gas:** If you detect the smell of gas, promptly cover the regulator with a wet towel, thick bed sheet, or gunny bag. This can help contain the gas leak and reduce its spread.
   - **Ventilate the Area:** Open all windows and doors to allow fresh air to circulate and disperse the gas. This helps lower the concentration of gas in the air and reduces the risk of ignition.
2. **Avoid Electrical Sparks**
   - **Do Not Use Electrical Switches:** Avoid touching any electrical switches, whether to turn them on or off. Electrical sparks can ignite the gas, leading to a potential explosion.
   - **Turn Off Electrical Devices:** If it is safe to do so, unplug any electrical devices that may pose a risk, but do not do so if it involves handling switches or cords.
3. **Alert Authorities**
   - **Contact the Gas Distributor/Fire Brigade:** Call the gas distributor or fire brigade immediately to report the leak. Provide them with detailed information about the situation, and follow their instructions.
   - **Evacuate the Area:** Ensure that all individuals in the vicinity are moved to a safe distance away from the suspected leak.
4. **Preventive Measures**
   - **Regular Maintenance:** Regularly inspect gas appliances and connections for leaks or damage. Ensure that gas cylinders and regulators are maintained in good condition.
   - **Proper Installation:** Ensure that all gas appliances and systems are installed by qualified professionals and adhere to safety regulations.

NAVIGATION

USE OF A COMPASS AND THE SIXTEEN POINTS OF A COMPASS

A compass is a crucial navigational instrument used to determine direction. It features a dial and a magnetic needle that pivots to align with the Earth's magnetic north, allowing users to identify other directions. The compass dial is marked with 360 degrees and divided into 16 points to indicate various directions. While North is often referenced as a starting point, any direction could be used for convenience. Explorers typically use degrees for precision instead of compass points. On a compass chart, directions are marked with numbers from 0 at North, looping back to 360 at North again. For example, east corresponds to 90 degrees, south to 180 degrees, and west to 270 degrees. Thus, instead of using abbreviations like S.E., one could specify 135 degrees.

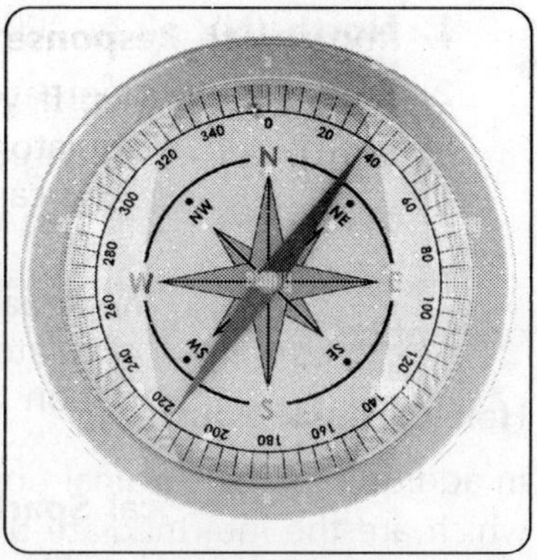

Compass

Finding direction is one of the essential skills of map making and map reading. Even the early man managed to find direction through the sun and stars. Later, the compass was invented.

Using a Compass

1. **Setting the Compass:** Rotate the compass so that the magnetic needle aligns with the north marking on the compass dial. This alignment is known as a compass setting.
2. **Finding Directions:** Place the compass on a flat, hard surface, and wait for the needle to stabilize. This will ensure accuracy. Do not use the compass near any sources of iron or metal, as they can interfere with the magnetic needle.
3. **Reading Degrees:** Besides cardinal and intermediate points, the compass dial is marked with degrees ranging from 0 to 360. For example, east is 90 degrees, south is 180 degrees, and west is 270 degrees. Directions can also be expressed in degrees, such as 135 degrees for southeast.

Cardinal Points

The compass is primarily divided into four cardinal points. Cardinal points are the four primary directions on a compass that provide the basic framework for navigation and orientation:

1. **North (N)** - 0 or 360 degrees
2. **East (E)** - 90 degrees
3. **South (S)** - 180 degrees
4. **West (W)** - 270 degrees

These are the main reference points used for navigation and orientation.

Half-Cardinal Points

In addition to the cardinal points, there are four half-cardinal points, which are the intermediate directions that lie halfway between each pair of cardinal points. They are:

1. **North-East (NE)** - 45 degrees
2. **South-East (SE)** - 135 degrees
3. **South-West (SW)** - 225 degrees
4. **North-West (NW)** - 315 degrees

Tertiary Points

The compass is further divided into eight tertiary points, these are the directions that lie halfway between each cardinal and half cardinal point. They provide more precise orientation and are used for finer navigation. They are:

1. **North-North-East (NNE)** - 22.5 degrees
2. **East-North-East (ENE)** - 67.5 degrees
3. **East-South-East (ESE)** - 112.5 degrees
4. **South-South-East (SSE)** - 157.5 degrees
5. **South-South-West (SSW)** - 202.5 degrees
6. **West-South-West (WSW)** - 247.5 degrees
7. **West-North-West (WNW)** - 292.5 degrees
8. **North-North-West (NNW)** - 337.5 degrees

LOCATING NORTH WITH THE HELP OF CONSTELLATIONS

1. **Introduction to Star Navigation:** Navigators use only a small fraction of the approximately 5,000 stars visible to the naked eye. These stars are grouped into constellations, which are not evenly distributed but form recognisable patterns across the night sky. The specific constellations visible depend on your geographic location, the time of year, and the hour of the night. As the Earth orbits the Sun and rotates on its axis, the night sky changes, causing constellations to appear to move in a circular path. Among these stars, the North Star, or Polaris, remains nearly fixed in the sky, making it a reliable point for navigation.
2. **The North Star:** The North Star is located less than 1° from true north and remains in a fixed position due to the Earth's axis pointing directly towards it. This star is part of the Little Dipper constellation and is the last star in the dipper's handle. To locate the North Star, use the two "pointer" stars in the Big Dipper constellation. By drawing an imaginary line through these stars and extending it approximately five times their distance, you will find the North Star. Despite being less bright than many other stars, its importance for navigation is unmatched due to its consistent position in the northern sky. However, the North Star is not visible in the southern hemisphere. As you move northward, Polaris rises higher in the sky, making it impractical for navigation above 70° latitude.
3. **Navigational Adjustments:** When using stars for navigation, it's essential to check the azimuth– the angle between the star and true north. A star near the northern horizon is useful for about half an hour. For southern travel, azimuth checks should be made every 15 minutes. When travelling east or west, challenges include stars rising too high in the sky or setting behind the horizon, requiring you to switch to another star. In the southern hemisphere, the Southern Cross is used similarly to Polaris for northern navigation. Understanding different constellation shapes and their global locations is crucial for effective star navigation.

4. **Recognisable Constellations:**
   - **The Big Dipper:** Also known as the Plough or Great Bear, the Big Dipper is an easily identifiable constellation in the northern hemisphere. It resembles a plough or dipper and is particularly useful for finding the north. The two stars in the Big Dipper's "handle" point towards the North Star. This constellation is crucial for scouts and other navigators as it helps locate true north.
   - **Orion:** This constellation represents a man with a sword and belt and is known for its distinctive alignment of three stars in a line, called the "belt," with three additional stars forming the "sword." Orion's belt and sword are visible from both hemispheres. The Zulus refer to these stars as the "Ingolubu," or three pigs pursued by three dogs, while the Masai tribe sees them as three bachelors followed by three old maids. To locate the North Star using Orion, extend a line from the centre star of Orion's belt through his head and continue it through two bright stars to find Polaris.

FOLLOWING A TRAIL

Understanding Compass Bearings & Distances

Compass bearings and distances are essential for effective trail navigation. Bearings, expressed in degrees, indicate the direction to travel from your current position to a point on the map, measured clockwise from the north. Distances are generally measured in metres or feet, and understanding how to measure these distances using the map's scale is crucial for estimating travel length and progress along the trail.

1. **Compass Bearings:** Bearings indicate the direction to travel from your current position to a specific point, measured in degrees clockwise from North. For example, a bearing of 065° denotes an angle of 65 degrees from the north. Accurate bearings are essential for precise navigation and orientation on the trail.

2. **Distance Measurement:** The distance on a map is determined using the scale provided. Distances are typically measured in metres or feet. Understanding how to translate the map's scale into real-world distances helps in planning and tracking your journey effectively.

Step-by-Step Guide to Following a Trail

1. **Plan Your Route:** Begin by studying the map to identify your trail, bearings, and distances. Mark key points and landmarks on the map to help with navigation.
2. **Set Your Compass:** Adjust the compass dial to align with the desired bearing. Ensure the compass is held level and steady for accurate readings.
3. **Orient the Map:** Place the map on a flat surface and align it with the compass so that the map's North matches the magnetic North indicated by the compass. This alignment helps ensure your route is correctly oriented.
4. **Follow the Bearing:** Use the compass to maintain the correct bearing while navigating. Adjust your direction as necessary to stay on course, and periodically compare your position with the map to ensure you are following the intended route.
5. **Measure Distances:** As you move along the trail, use the map's scale to measure the distance covered. This helps you track your progress and ensures you are travelling the intended distance.
6. **Navigate Obstacles:** Be prepared to adjust your bearing or route if you encounter obstacles. Use visible landmarks or map features to navigate around any difficulties and continue on the trail.

Compass and Tools

- **Pace:** A pace, also known as a double-pace or passus, is an ancient Roman measure of distance equivalent to the length of two full strides. One pace, or passus, equals approximately 1.48 metres or 58.1 inches. In modern terms, a pace is often considered as 30 inches. Pacing helps in estimating distances travelled by counting each heel strike or every other step.

- **Prismatic Compass:** A prismatic compass is a tool for taking accurate bearings. To use it, hold the compass level and steady, ensuring the card swings freely. Align the sighting slit with the target object, and read the bearing from the compass card through the prism. Accurate bearings can be read with precision, typically to within 10 miles.

IMPORTANT TERMS

SCALE

The scale of a map is a critical concept in cartography that determines the relationship between distances on the map and actual distances on the ground. Understanding this helps in interpreting the map accurately and planning routes.

- **Ratio/Representative Fraction (RF):** The scale is often expressed as a ratio or fraction, such as 1:100,000. This means that 1 unit on the map equals 100,000 of the same units on the ground. For instance:
  - **1:100,000 Scale:** 1 centimetre on the map represents 1 kilometre (100,000 centimetres) on the ground.
  - **1:25,000 Scale:** 1 centimetre on the map equals 250 metres on the ground.
  - **1:1,000,000 Scale:** 1 centimetre on the map equals 10 kilometres on the ground.
  - **Large Scale Maps** (e.g., 1:10,000) show more detail but cover a smaller area.
  - **Small Scale Maps** (e.g., 1:250,000) cover a larger area but with less detail.
- **Verbal Scale:** A verbal scale describes the relationship between map and ground distances in words. This is a descriptive statement indicating map distances. Examples include:
  - **"1 inch equals 1 mile":** Each inch on the map represents one mile on the ground.
  - **"1 centimetre equals 10 kilometres":** Each centimetre on the map represents 10 kilometres on the ground.

- Verbal scales provide an intuitive understanding but are less precise if the map is resized.

- **Graphic Scale:** A visual representation often displayed as a bar or line marked with the distance corresponding to units of measurement on the map. It is useful for measuring distances directly on the map. It remains accurate if the map size changes, unlike the ratio or verbal scales.
- **Using a Graphic Scale:** Align a ruler with the graphic scale to measure distances on the map. The scale often includes both metric and imperial units and is useful for direct distance measurement.

Large Scale vs. Small Scale

- **Large Scale Maps:** Show more detail because the representative fraction is smaller (e.g., 1:10,000). They cover a smaller area but provide detailed information.
- **Small Scale Maps:** Cover larger areas but with less detail due to a larger representative fraction (e.g., 1:250,000). They are useful for broader overviews.

DIRECTION

Direction involves determining and following bearings, which are critical for navigation and orienting oneself on a map.

- **Cardinal Points:** These are the four main directions on a compass:
  - **North (N):** 0° or 360°
  - **East (E):** 90°
  - **South (S):** 180°
  - **West (W):** 270°
- **Intermediate Points: These include:**
  - **North-East (NE):** 45°
  - **South-East (SE):** 135°
  - **South-West (SW):** 225°
  - **North-West (NW):** 315°

- **Bearings:** Bearings are measured in degrees from North, moving clockwise:
  - ❑ **True Bearing:** The angle measured in degrees from the north to a point or object. For example, a bearing of 065° indicates that the direction is 65 degrees to the east of the north.
  - ❑ **Forward Bearing:** The same as true bearing, used to describe the direction of travel.

CONVENTIONAL SIGNS

Conventional signs on maps use symbols and colours to represent various features and information in a clear and concise manner. Symbols simplify the map, making it easier to read and interpret without cluttering the space with text. Provides a standardised way of representing features, ensuring uniform understanding.

Types of Symbols

- **Colour Codes:**
  - ❑ **Blue:** Represents water bodies such as rivers, lakes, and ponds.
  - ❑ **Green:** Indicates vegetation such as forests and parks.
  - ❑ **Brown:** Shows contour lines, mountain ranges, and other landforms.
  - ❑ **Red:** Used for roads, boundaries, and other important features.
- **Shape Symbols:**
  - ❑ **Squares/Circles:** Represent buildings, towns, or points of interest.
  - ❑ **Lines:** Depict roads, trails, and boundaries.
- **Legend:** Also known as the map key, this section explains the meaning of each symbol and colour used on the map. It acts as a dictionary for interpreting the map's symbols.

CONTOURS

Contours are lines on a map that connect points of equal elevation. They are essential for understanding the topography and terrain of an area. It helps in understanding the terrain, planning routes, and navigating difficult landscapes.

- **Contour Lines:** Show the shape and elevation of the land. For example:
  - **Close Spacing:** Indicates steep terrain, such as a mountain.
  - **Wide Spacing:** Indicates gentle slopes, like rolling hills.
  - **Closed circles:** Represent hills or peaks, while V-shaped lines often denote valleys.
- **Contour Interval:** The vertical distance between adjacent contour lines. For instance, a contour interval of 50 metres means that each line represents a 50-metre elevation change. Smaller intervals provide more detailed topographical information. It helps gauge the steepness of the terrain and plan routes accordingly.

GRID REFERENCE

Grid reference systems help locate specific points on a map using a grid of lines. It is useful for identifying locations, coordinating search and rescue operations, and providing detailed navigation.

- **Grid System:** Maps are divided into a grid of squares or cells using horizontal and vertical lines. Each square is identified by a combination of letters and numbers, such as "A5" or "C8".
- **Using Grid References:**
  - **Identify the Grid Square:** Locate the grid square by matching the letters and numbers on the map.
  - **Precise Location:** This helps in finding exact positions and navigating accurately.

TOURIST MAPS

Tourist maps are specialised maps designed to assist travellers in navigating and exploring a region. They highlight key points of interest, amenities, and travel routes.

Features of Tourist Maps

- **Landmarks and Attractions:** Tourist maps prominently mark popular attractions such as historical sites, monuments, museums, parks, and cultural landmarks. These are often highlighted with symbols or icons for easy identification.
- **Tourist Services:** Important facilities such as hotels, restaurants, hospitals, and transportation hubs (bus stations, train stations) are clearly marked. These symbols help travellers find essential services quickly.
- **Scale and Orientation:** The scale on a tourist map helps determine distances between locations. Orientation is typically shown with a compass rose or north arrow to help users understand map direction. Some maps include a graphic scale bar for precise measurement.
- **Symbols and Icons:** Tourist maps use various symbols and icons to represent different types of locations and services. For example, a fork and knife icon might indicate restaurants, while a bed icon could denote hotels. A legend explains what each symbol means.
- **Routes and Trails:** Maps may include walking routes, sightseeing trails, and public transport routes to guide travellers through popular areas. This helps in planning a visit or navigating through a city.
- **Detailed Insets:** Larger tourist maps might include inset maps for specific areas of interest, such as city centres or major tourist spots, providing a more detailed view of these areas.

Effective Map Reading

- **Understand the Legend:** Before using the map, familiarise yourself with the legend or key to understand the meaning of various symbols and colors. This ensures you can accurately interpret the information presented.
- **Check the scale:** Pay attention to the scale of the map to estimate distances accurately. If the map has a graphic scale, use it to measure real-world distances by aligning it with your route.

- **Orient the Map:** Align the map with the actual direction you're facing. Use the compass rose or north arrow to ensure that the map is oriented correctly. This helps with accurate navigation and route planning.
- **Plan Your Route:** Identify key landmarks, services, and routes before you start your journey. Mark your starting point and destination, and plan the best route based on the map's features.
- **Use Landmarks:** Look for prominent landmarks and use them as reference points to navigate. This helps you stay oriented and ensures you're on the right path.
- **Stay Aware of Your Surroundings:** While using the map, keep an eye on your surroundings. This helps in cross-referencing the map with real-world features and avoiding disorientation.

FIRST AID

BURNS AND SCALDS

Burns can result from heat, chemicals, or friction. **Scalds** are specifically caused by moist heat, such as boiling water, steam, or hot oil.

Minor Burns

Symptoms: Pain, redness, and sometimes blisters in a small area.

Management

- **Cool the Burn:** Immediately immerse the affected area in cold water for at least 10 minutes. This helps to relieve pain and prevent further skin damage. Avoid using ice directly on the burn, as it can worsen the injury.
- **Clean the Area:** Gently wash the burn with a diluted antiseptic solution (such as Dettol diluted with water) to prevent infection. Avoid pricking blisters, as they act as a protective layer.
- **Cover the Burn:** Use sterile gauze to cover the burn. Initially, there may be a lot of oozing, so ensure the padding is ample to absorb any discharge and protect the area.
- **Severe Burns:** For severe burns affecting large areas of the body or causing deep tissue damage, seek immediate medical attention.

SPRAINS

A sprain occurs when ligaments around a joint are stretched or torn, commonly seen in the ankle.

Symptoms: Pain, swelling, and difficulty moving the affected joint. Distinguishing a sprain from a fracture can be challenging.

Management

- **Assess the Injury:** If there was a significant impact or blow to the joint, it might be a fracture. In such cases, treat the injury as if it were a fracture until a proper medical evaluation is available.
- **Rest and Elevate:** Rest the affected joint and keep it elevated to reduce swelling.
- **Apply Ice:** Use ice packs wrapped in a cloth to reduce swelling and pain. Apply ice for 15-20 minutes every hour as needed.
- **Compression:** Apply an elastic bandage to the injured area to provide compression and reduce swelling. Ensure the bandage is snug but not too tight.
- **Seek Medical Advice:** For severe pain, inability to move the joint, or significant swelling, seek medical attention to rule out a fracture and receive appropriate care.

STINGS AND BITES

Stings: Typically from insects such as bees.

Management

- **Remove the Sting:** If the sting is still present, use the point of a sterilised needle or a pair of tweezers to gently scrape it out. Avoid squeezing the sting sac to prevent injecting more venom.
- **Apply Treatment:** Use a solution of washing soda or apply antiseptic spirit to the area to neutralise the venom and reduce pain.
- **Cover the Area:** Apply a dry dressing to protect the area from infection and further irritation.

- **Inside the Mouth:** If the sting is in the mouth, rinse with a solution of bicarbonate soda (two teaspoonfuls to a pint of water). Apply a hot compress to the front of the neck to ease discomfort.

Bites: For insect bites, clean the area with soap and water, apply an antiseptic, and cover with a sterile dressing.

USE OF A TRIANGULAR BANDAGE FOR VARIOUS INJURIES

Triangular bandages are versatile and can be used for various types of injuries, including bandaging the head, hand, knee, foot, ankle, and supporting a fractured arm.

Triangular bandages can be used in the following ways for different body parts:

Head Bandage

- **Positioning:** Stand behind the casualty and use the triangular bandage as a whole cloth with a narrow hem folded along the base.
- **Placement:** Place the centre of the base in the middle of the forehead, close to the eyebrows.
- **Securing:** Bring the point over the top of the head to cover the dressing and down the back of the head. Cross over the point and bring the ends around the head to the front.
- **Tying:** Tie the ends together using a reef knot low on the forehead.
- **Adjusting:** Steady the head with one hand and gently pull the point down to apply the desired amount of pressure to the dressing. Fold the point up towards the top of the head and secure it with a safety pin, or tuck it under the back crisscross.

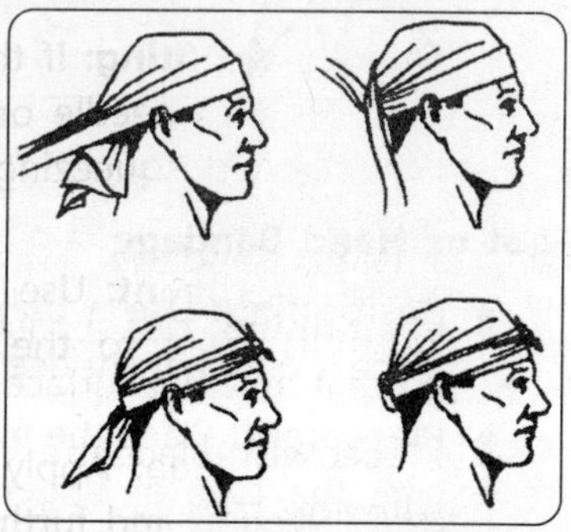

Head Bandage

Knee or Elbow Bandage

- **Positioning:** Use a triangular bandage as a whole cloth with a narrow hem folded along the base.
- **Placement:** Place the centre of the base on the leg below the kneecap with the point towards the top of the leg, or on the forearm with the point towards the shoulder for an elbow bandage.
- **Securing:** Bring the ends around the joint, crossing over the point in front of the elbow or at the back of the knee.
- **Tying:** Bring the ends up and tie off over the point.
- **Adjusting:** Pull the point up to apply the right amount of pressure to the dressing, then fold it down and secure it with a safety pin or tuck it under the knot.

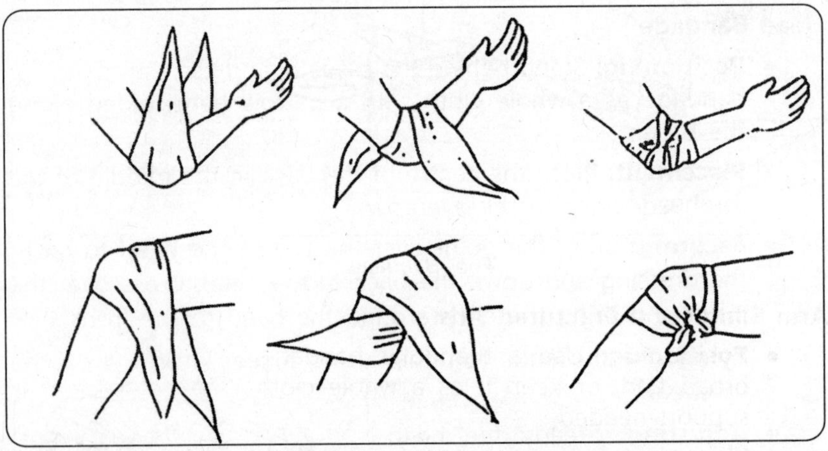

Knee or Elbow Bandage

Foot or Hand Bandage

- **Positioning:** Use a triangular bandage as a whole cloth and place it on a flat surface with the point away from the casualty.
- **Placement:** Place the foot or hand on the triangular bandage with the toes or fingers towards the point, leaving enough bandage at the ankle or wrist to fully cover the part.

(2807) S&G (E)—9-II

- **Securing:** Bring the point up and over the foot or hand to rest on the lower leg or wrist. Bring the ends alongside the foot or hand, and crisscross the folded ends up and around the ankle or wrist.
- **Tying:** Cross over the point and wrap any extra bandage before tying it off over the point.
- **Adjusting:** If the point extends beyond the knot, pull it up to apply the desired pressure, fold it downward, and tuck under the knot.

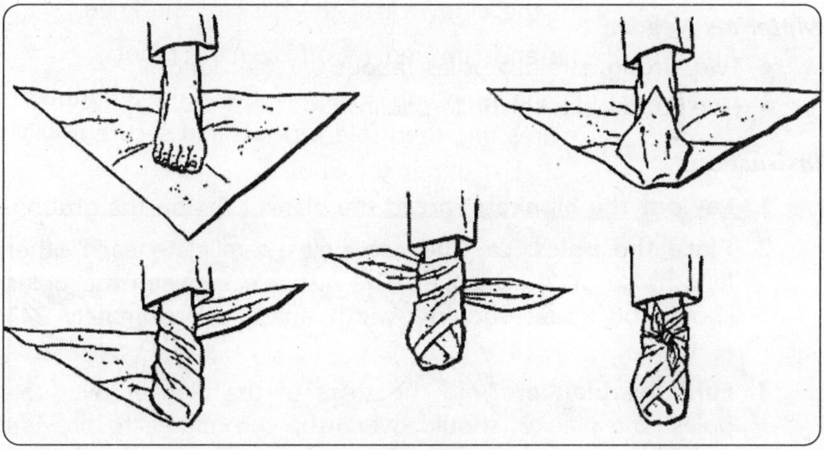

Foot Bandage

Arm Sling for a Fractured Arm

- **Positioning:** Use a triangular bandage and fold it into a broad fold, or keep it as a whole cloth, depending on the support needed.
- **Placement:** Place the bandage under the arm, ensuring that the point is towards the elbow and the base is along the forearm.
- **Securing:** Bring the ends up over the shoulder on the opposite side.
- **Tying:** Tie the ends securely around the neck, ensuring the arm is supported in a comfortable position.
- **Adjusting:** Ensure the knot is positioned at the side of the neck to avoid pressure on the spine. Adjust the bandage for comfort, and secure any loose ends with a safety pin.

- Using a triangular bandage correctly can provide necessary support and protection for various injuries, making it a crucial skill for first aiders.

IMPROVISED STRETCHER

Creating an improvised stretcher is an essential skill for Scouts and Guides. Three methods to create a stretcher using commonly available materials are:

Method 1: Using Two Poles and a Blanket

Materials Needed

- Two strong, straight poles (about 6-7 feet long)
- One sturdy blanket or tarpaulin

Instructions

1. **Lay out the blanket:** Spread the blanket flat on the ground.
2. **Place the poles:** Lay the two poles parallel to each other lengthwise on the blanket. The distance between the poles should be about shoulder-width apart (approximately 2-3 feet).
3. **Fold the blanket:** Fold the sides of the blanket over the poles. The blanket should overlap in the middle to provide a double layer of support.
4. **Secure the Blanket:** Roll the edges of the blanket around the poles for additional strength. Ensure the blanket is tightly wrapped around the poles and there is enough overlap to hold the weight of the injured person securely.
5. **Check Stability:** Ensure the blanket is securely wrapped around the poles and that the poles are strong enough to support the weight of the injured person. Test it by gently pressing down in the middle to check for any signs of weakness.

Method 2: Using Shirts and Poles

Materials Needed

- Two strong, straight poles (about 6-7 feet long)
- Four long-sleeved shirts

Instructions

1. **Prepare the shirts:** Button up the shirts completely and turn them inside out.
2. **Thread the Poles:** Thread one pole through the sleeves of two shirts, and the other pole through the sleeves of the other two shirts. Space the shirts evenly along the poles.
3. **Secure the shirts:** Pull the body of each shirt over the pole to ensure they are tightly secured and provide a sturdy base. Make sure the sleeves are fully extended and not bunched up.
4. **Check Stability:** Ensure the shirts are securely wrapped around the poles and that the poles are strong enough to support the weight of the injured person. Test it by gently pressing down in the middle to check for any signs of weakness.

Method 3: Using Ropes and Poles

Materials Needed

- Two strong, straight poles (about 6-7 feet long)
- Strong ropes or cords (at least 20-30 feet)

Instructions

1. **Place the poles:** Lay the two poles parallel to each other on the ground, about shoulder-width apart.
2. **Create the base:** Start by tying one end of the rope to one pole at about waist height. Weave the rope back and forth between the poles, creating a sturdy net-like structure. The spacing between the rope weaves should be no more than a few inches.
3. **Secure the rope:** Once you have woven the rope to cover the necessary length (about 5-6 feet), tie the end of the rope securely to the other pole. Ensure that each end of the rope is tightly secured and that the rope is taut and does not sag.
4. **Check Stability:** Ensure that the woven rope is tightly secured and that the poles are strong enough to support the weight of the injured person. Test it by gently pressing down in the middle to check for any signs of weakness.

Tips for Using the Improvised Stretcher

- **Stability and Comfort:** Ensure the stretcher is stable and comfortable for the injured person. Adjust the materials as necessary to avoid discomfort or additional injury.
- **Lifting and Carrying:** When lifting and carrying the stretcher, coordinate movements with your team to avoid jostling the injured person. Lift smoothly and evenly, and communicate clearly with all carriers.
- **Safety First:** Always prioritise the safety of the injured person and the rescuers. Ensure the stretcher can bear the weight and is securely assembled. Regularly check the stability of the stretcher during transport.
- **Minimise Movement:** Minimise the movement of the injured person as much as possible to prevent further injury. Secure the injured person with additional ropes or straps, if necessary.
- **Use Additional Padding:** If available, use additional padding, such as extra clothing or soft materials, to provide comfort and reduce the risk of pressure points.

ESTIMATION

JUDGING DISTANCES AND WIDTHS

- **Using a Rope:** A rope marked with centimetres or inches can help estimate short distances. Simply place the rope along the ground to gauge how far a certain point is.
- **Using Your Hand:** Spread your thumb and little finger as wide as possible and use this span to estimate short distances. This can be helpful when determining the distance between objects nearby.
- **Using a Staff:** A staff marked with measurements (such as inches or centimetres) can be used for estimating short distances. While this is useful for practice, it should not be used during tests for precise measurement.

KNOWING THE LENGTH OF YOUR STRIDE/PACE FOR DISTANCE ESTIMATION

To estimate long distances, knowing the length of your stride or pace is important. Measure the distance you cover in one stride and count the steps as you walk. Multiply the number of steps by your stride length to estimate the total distance.

SHORT AND LONG DISTANCES

Estimating Short Distances:

1. **Using a Rope:** A rope marked with measurements can be used for estimating short lengths.
2. **Using Your Hand:** You can estimate distances between objects using the span of your hand (thumb to little finger).
3. **Using a Staff:** A staff with measurements can also be helpful for estimating short distances, ideal for practice but not during actual tests.

Estimating Long Distances:

1. **Using Your Pace:** First, determine the length of your stride. Walk a known distance (like 5 metres) and count the number of paces. Multiply the number of paces by your stride length to estimate longer distances.

   Example: If you take 8 steps to cover 5 metres, your stride length is 5 metres / 8 steps = 0.625 metres per step. If you take 40 steps, the estimated distance is 40 steps × 0.625 metres = 25 metres.
2. **Using a Rope:** For more accuracy, a long rope can be used to estimate longer distances.
3. **Using a Bicycle:** Count the number of pedal rotations it takes to cover a distance. This can also be used to estimate longer distances.

ESTIMATING DISTANCE ACROSS A RIVER

Using Pacing:

- Identify an object (e.g., a tree) on the opposite bank of the river.
- Walk perpendicular to the line between you and the object, counting your paces.

- Continue walking in the same direction, then walk inland to align with the object again. The number of steps inland will give you an approximate distance across the river.

Using a Sighting Stick:

- Hold a stick at arm's length and measure the height of an object in the distance.
- **Apply the formula:**
    - ❑ Distance = (Height of object × Length of your arm) / Height on stick.
    - ❑ This helps estimate the distance to the object.

MEASURING WIDTHS

1. **Napoleon Hat Brim Method:** Stand on the shore and hold your hand (or a hat) to your forehead, looking at the opposite shore. Move your hand or hat to estimate the width of the river, then pace the distance to calculate it.
2. **Stride/Step Method:** Mark a spot perpendicular to the river and walk several paces to a new point. The distance between these points can give you the width of the river.
3. **Compass Method:** Use a compass to align with a distant object across the river and calculate the width based on the direction and distance you walk.

FACTORS AFFECTING PERCEPTION OF DISTANCE

When estimating distances, various factors can affect how we perceive the size or distance of objects.

Objects Appear Farther

1. **In the Shade:** When objects are in shadow, they can appear more distant due to the contrast between light and dark areas.
2. **Across a Valley:** The distance between you and an object across a valley often seems greater due to the visual separation.

3. **Same Colour as the Background:** Objects that match the colour of their surroundings may appear farther away, as there is less contrast to define their boundaries.
4. **In a Heat Haze:** A heat haze, which occurs on hot days with rising heat waves, can make distant objects appear blurry and farther away.
5. **Lying Down or Kneeling:** From a lower vantage point (like lying down or kneeling), distances often seem longer because your horizon is limited.

Objects Appear Closer

1. **With the Sun Behind You:** When the sun is behind you, it often creates sharper contrasts and makes objects seem closer and more defined.
2. **In Very Clear Air:** On days with clear, crisp air, objects often appear closer because there are no particles or haze to obscure the view.
3. **Different Colour Background:** Objects stand out more when placed against a contrasting background, making them seem closer.
4. **On Flat Ground or Snow-Covered Terrain:** A flat, uniform surface or snow can make distances seem shorter because there's no change in terrain to disrupt the view.
5. **When Larger than Nearby Objects:** If an object is significantly larger than others in the area, it can create the illusion of being closer, as our brains associate size with proximity.
6. **Across Water or a Deep Valley:** Water and valleys can create a visual depth that pulls objects into sharper focus, making them seem closer.
7. **At Night:** Objects at night often appear closer than they do during the day because of the lack of other visual reference points (e.g., sunlight) that can make them seem farther away.

OUTDOOR ACTIVITIES

PARTICIPATE IN A TROOP-WIDE GAME

Troop-wide games particularly night games are an integral and enjoyable part of Scouting, offering opportunities for Scouts to develop various skills and overcome fears through imaginative and engaging activities. Benefits of participating in these games are as follows:

1. **Overcoming Fear of the Dark:** Many Scouts develop confidence and reduce their fear of the dark through gradual training in "Night Scouting."

   Engaging in activities during the night helps Scouts become more comfortable in low-light conditions. Gradual training helps them overcome any fears they may have about the dark.

2. **Skill Enhancement:** Scouts improve their observational and memory skills by completing tasks such as making a sketch map of a strange village in the dark without asking questions.

   Engaging in imaginative scenarios like bank robberies, spies, and rocket missions boosts problem-solving and critical thinking abilities.

Preparing for Night Games

- **Cooperation with authorities:** Inform local police and other interested parties about the night games to avoid misunderstandings.

  The police may even cooperate and assist with the games, adding an element of realism and safety.

- **Daylight Training:** Initial training can be conducted during the day using masks that limit vision to simulate night conditions without complete blindness.

  This helps Scouts adjust gradually to operating in low-light environments.

- **Weather and Moonlight considerations:** Check the weather forecast and the phase of the moon before planning night games.

  Some games may require complete darkness, while others might benefit from a bit of moonlight.

Planning and Reconnaissance

- **Ground Familiarity:** Scout the game area in daylight to understand the boundaries and ensure the terrain is familiar to the participants, especially patrol leaders. This helps in setting clear and manageable boundaries for the game.
- **Game Duration:** Night games should typically last 45 to 60 minutes, depending on the area used and the number of participants. This duration keeps Scouts engaged and focused without becoming overly tired or bored.

Importance of a clear background story

- **Engagement through Storytelling:** A good story can significantly enhance the game's immersion and engagement.

  Keep the story simple and clear to ensure everyone understands and participates actively.
- **Realism in Instructions:** Translate the story into realistic instructions and actions for the Scouts.

  For example, instead of just saying a scout is guarding idols, specify that he is guarding an area marked by four oak trees containing old signalling flags.

Examples of Night Games

Spies in Camp

Objective: One patrol, acting as spies, must infiltrate the camp and place a piece of firewood on the campfire without being caught by the guards (other patrols).

Preparation:

- Select a suitable area for the campfire and mark a boundary around it.
- Equip spies with pieces of firewood and distinguish them with white bands.
- Brief both spies and guards on the game rules and objectives.

Execution:

- Spies take positions at an agreed-upon distance from the camp.
- On the signal, spies try to sneak into the camp and place their firewood on the fire.
- Guards patrol the boundary and try to capture spies by taking their firewood.
- Successful spies remain by the fire, while captured spies are out of the game.

Night Scavenger Hunt

Objective: Patrols compete to find and collect a list of specific items within a set time.

Preparation:

- Create a list of items that are a mix of nature study, creativity, and teamwork challenges.
- Examples include: a baked potato, a pound of pebbles in a paper bag, a beggar man's knot, a white maple leaf, the signature of the village policeman, one of the Scoutmaster's shoes, a kidnapped and bound member of another patrol, a whittled doll, a moth, five named wildflowers, a feather over three inches long, and items borrowed from a non-Scout.

Execution:

- Patrols are given the list and a time limit to find as many items as possible.
- Items must be collected and brought back to a designated area.
- Points are awarded based on the number of items found and their completeness.
- The patrol with the most points at the end of the game wins.

Key Points for Successful Night Games

- **Clear Instructions:** Ensure all participants understand the game rules and objectives before starting to avoid confusion and ensure active participation.

- **Active Participation:** Games should involve real action to keep scouts engaged. Avoid long periods of inactivity to maintain interest and enthusiasm.
- **Leadership and Teamwork:** Night games provide excellent opportunities for Scouts to develop leadership and teamwork skills, crucial for their overall development in Scouting.

By carefully planning and executing night games, Scouts can gain invaluable skills, build confidence, and have a lot of fun in the process, making Scouting a memorable and enriching experience.

PARTICIPATE IN A TROOP CAMPFIRE

A troop campfire is a cherished tradition that offers scouts a chance to relax and bond around a fire. It's an opportunity to share stories, sing songs, and perform skits, which fosters a sense of community and tradition among scouts.

How to participate

- **Preparation:** Bring along any items you might need for your contribution, such as musical instruments, costumes, or props for skits. Make sure you dress appropriately for the weather and wear warm clothing if it's chilly.
- **Engagement:** Actively participate in the activities planned for the campfire. This might include singing along to campfire songs, telling a favourite story, or taking part in a skit. Engagement helps create a lively and enjoyable atmosphere.
- **Safety and Respect:** Follow all safety guidelines related to the campfire. Stay a safe distance from the flames and listen to instructions from the leaders. Show respect for others' performances and be attentive during the campfire activities.

Examples

- **Campfire Songs:** Participate in singing traditional campfire songs, which often involve call-and-response or group participation.
- **Skits:** Perform or watch short, humorous skits. These skits are usually lighthearted and designed to entertain the troop.

ROAD SAFETY RULES FOR VEHICLES

Understanding and practicing road safety rules is crucial for preventing accidents and ensuring safe travel for all road users. Understanding and adhering to road safety rules is crucial for preventing accidents and ensuring the safety of everyone on the road. These rules help manage traffic flow and protect both drivers and pedestrians.

Key Rules

- **Obey traffic signals and signs:** Traffic signals and signs are designed to manage traffic flow and ensure safety. Always follow these signals to avoid accidents and ensure smooth traffic movement.
- **Use Seatbelts:** Seatbelts are essential for protecting passengers in the event of a crash. Ensure that everyone in the vehicle is wearing a seatbelt before starting your journey.
- **Adhere to speed limits:** Speed limits are set to ensure safety on different types of roads and conditions. Always drive within these limits and adjust your speed based on road conditions, weather, and traffic.
- **Avoid Distractions:** Focus on driving and avoid distractions such as using your phone or eating while driving. Staying focused helps you respond quickly to any hazards.
- **Respect Pedestrians:** Always yield to pedestrians at crosswalks, and be vigilant in areas where people frequently cross the road. This helps ensure their safety and prevent accidents.

Practicing Road Safety

- **Pedestrian Awareness:** Practice awareness of pedestrian areas and signals to ensure you respect their right of way.
- **Driver Responsibilities:** If you're a driver, regularly check your vehicle's condition and practice safe driving habits.

INFORMATION ABOUT RIDING A BICYCLE

Riding a bicycle is an enjoyable and practical mode of transportation. Knowing how to ride a bicycle safely involves learning the skills needed for cycling and understanding how to handle a bike in different conditions.

Key Skills

- **Wear a helmet:** Always wear a properly fitted helmet to protect your head in case of a fall or accident. It is one of the most important safety measures for cyclists.
- **Bike Maintenance:** Regularly check your bike's brakes, tyres, and gears to ensure they are functioning correctly. Proper maintenance helps prevent breakdowns and ensures a smooth ride.
- **Follow traffic rules:** Ride your bicycle in the direction of traffic, obey traffic signals, and use hand signals to indicate turns or stops. This helps you stay safe and be predictable to other road users.
- **Be Visible:** Wear bright clothing and use bike lights or reflectors, especially if you're riding in low-light conditions. This increases your visibility and reduces the risk of accidents.
- **Stay Alert:** Pay attention to your surroundings while riding, watch for obstacles, and avoid distractions. Being aware of your environment helps you react quickly to potential hazards.

Practicing Cycling Skills

- **Balance and Control:** Practice starting, stopping, and steering in a safe, open area to build your confidence and control.
- **Road Awareness:** Ride in areas that are safe and suitable for cycling, and be mindful of other road users and potential hazards.

VISIT A FACTORY TO UNDERSTAND THE MANUFACTURING PROCESS

A factory visit provides valuable insights into how products are made and the processes involved in manufacturing. It's an opportunity to learn about industrial operations and see machinery in action. Gain insight into how products are made and appreciate the importance of different types of work. It helps you understand the effort and skill required for different types of labour.

Following are things the scouts and guides can observe:

- **Learn about the factory:** Research the factory and the types of products they manufacture. Understand the basics of their production process.
- **Respect Factory Rules:** Follow all safety protocols and guidelines provided by the factory staff. Wear any required protective gear.
- **Observe the process:** Watch how raw materials are transformed into finished products. Pay attention to the machinery and steps involved.
- **Ask Questions:** Don't hesitate to ask questions about the manufacturing process. Factory staff can provide valuable insights and answer your queries about the production methods.
- **Respect the Dignity of Labour:** Appreciate the work of factory employees and understand the skill and effort involved in the manufacturing process.
- **Examples of factory visits:** Assembly Line: Observe how products are assembled step by step and understand the roles of different workers in the process.
- **Quality Control:** Learn about the checks and tests that ensure products meet quality standards and are safe for use.

SERVICE

As part of the Dwitiya Sopan (Second Stage) in Bharat Scouts and Guides, scouts and guides are required to complete one of the following service activities. Each option emphasises community service, social responsibility, and environmental stewardship.

UNDERTAKING A DEVELOPMENT PROJECT IN A SCHOOL OR COMMUNITY

Objective: Identify a need or improvement area within your school and work on a project to address it.

Steps

- **Consultation:** Discuss potential projects with the head of your institution to ensure alignment with school priorities.

- **Planning:** Develop a detailed plan outlining the project scope, objectives, required resources, and timeline.
- **Implementation:** Carry out the project, involving fellow Scouts and other students if possible. This could include activities such as creating a school garden, improving school infrastructure, or organising educational workshops.
- **Evaluation:** After completion, evaluate the project's impact and document the process and results.

PARTICIPATING IN A SOCIAL SERVICE CAMP

Objective: Engage in sustained community service through participation in social service camps.

Steps

- **Selection:** Choose a social service camp organised by Bharat Scouts and Guides or any other recognised organisation.
- **Participation:** Actively participate in the camp activities, which could include helping in medical camps, literacy programmes, or environmental conservation efforts.
- **Documentation:** Maintain a record of your participation, noting the activities performed, the skills learned, and the impact made.

SERVING AT A COMMUNITY FAIR OR MELA

Objective: Support the organisation and execution of a community event, such as a fair or mela.

Steps

- **Preparation:** Assist in the preparatory activities such as setting up stalls, arranging logistics, and coordinating with vendors.
- **During the event,** help manage the event by guiding visitors, maintaining order, and assisting with any required tasks.
- **Post-Event:** Participate in the cleanup and dismantling activities, ensuring the venue is returned to its original state.

PARTICIPATING IN AN ANTI-LITTER CAMPAIGN

Objective: Promote cleanliness and environmental consciousness by conducting an anti-litter campaign.

Steps

- **Planning:** Identify a littered area around your school or Scout headquarters. Plan the cleanup campaign with your patrol, deciding on tasks and responsibilities.
- **Execution:** Conduct the cleanup drive, collecting litter, segregating waste, and disposing of it responsibly.
- **Awareness:** Educate the community about the importance of keeping the area clean and encourage sustainable practices to prevent future littering.

DEMONSTRATING THE 3 R'S OF CONSERVATION (REDUCE, RECYCLE, REUSE)

Objective: Promote sustainable living by demonstrating the principles of Reduce, Recycle, and Reuse.

Steps

- **Education:** Learn about the 3 R's and how they can be applied in daily life. Share this knowledge with your patrol and community.
- **Projects:** Implement projects that embody the 3R's, such as creating compost from organic waste, setting up recycling bins, or crafting items from reusable materials.
- **Advocacy:** Encourage others to adopt these practices through workshops, presentations, or community events.

FORMING AND PARTICIPATING IN SELF HELP GROUPS

Objective: Establish or join a self-help group to support community initiatives and promote collective growth.

Steps

- **Formation:** Collaborate with peers and community members to form a self-help group focused on a specific cause or need.
- **Activities:** Engage in group activities that may include skill development workshops, income-generating projects, or social welfare programmes.

- **Impact:** Measure and document the group's contributions to the community and the benefits derived from collective action.

SENSE TRAINING

KIM'S GAMES

Kim's Games are designed to sharpen sensory skills and memory, drawing inspiration from Rudyard Kipling's novel "Kim," where the protagonist enhances his perceptual abilities. These games focus on training different senses: vision, hearing, taste, smell, and touch, providing valuable practice in observation and recall. They are suitable for all ages and help identify any unnoticed sensory deficiencies.

OBSERVATION GAME

The observation game, central to Kim's games, is a powerful tool for enhancing visual memory and attention to detail. To set up this game, the Scoutmaster arranges a variety of items on a tray—such as knives, spoons, pencils, pens, stones, and books—ensuring there are no more than fifteen items to keep the challenge manageable for beginners. These items are then covered with cloth. Players sit around the tray where they can see it, and the Scoutmaster uncovers the tray for one minute. During this brief period, players must closely observe and memorise as many items as possible. After the tray is covered again, players write down all the items they can recall. Alternatively, the scoutmaster can use a pre-made list of items and mark off what players remember as they whisper their guesses. The player who recalls the most items correctly wins the game. This exercise not only improves memory but also fosters attention to detail and enhances observational skills.

TASTE GAMES

Taste games offer a fun and engaging way to train the sense of taste while being mindful of food allergies. To conduct this game, select 10-12 items with distinct flavours—such as different types of fruits, sauces, or spices. Players are blindfolded to eliminate visual cues and given a toothpick dipped in each flavour or a small sample to taste. After tasting each item, players write down what they think it is. This game challenges participants to use their sense of taste to identify various foods, honing their ability to discern subtle differences in flavor. Ensuring that all participants are aware of potential food allergies and sensitivities is crucial for a safe and enjoyable experience.

SOUND GAMES

Sound games are designed to enhance auditory perception and memory. To prepare for this game, create a playlist of various sounds using an MP3 player. You can find rights-free sound effects on various websites or use familiar sounds from the meeting place, such as doors creaking, keys jingling, or footsteps. During the game, players cover their eyes and listen to each sound. After the sounds are played, players write down what they heard or try to recall all the sounds from the playlist. For a more challenging variation, use shakers filled with different objects (e.g., rice, beans, paper clips) and have players match containers that produce the same sound or identify the objects inside. This game improves listening skills and helps players differentiate between various auditory cues.

SMELLING GAMES

Smelling games are excellent for developing the sense of smell. To set up this game, prepare 10-12 small containers with strong-smelling substances, such as vinegar, coffee, or hot sauce. Cover the containers with a piece of sponge to prevent players from seeing the contents. Players take turns smelling each container and writing down what they believe they are detecting. This activity challenges participants to use their sense of smell to identify different scents and enhances their ability to recognise and recall odors. The game can be adapted for various difficulty levels by choosing more or less distinctive smells.

TOUCH GAMES

Touch games focus on improving tactile perception and memory. To create a touch-based game, prepare small pouches of opaque fabric that are thick enough to conceal the contents but thin enough to feel through. Place small, non-perishable items in each pouch, such as paper clips, Lego pieces, or keys, and number the pouches for reference. Players sit in a circle and pass the pouches around, feeling each one and trying to identify the item inside based on touch alone. Alternatively, use larger or messier items in paper or non-transparent plastic bags and have players guess the item by feeling it. This game enhances the ability to distinguish different textures and shapes, fostering a greater awareness of tactile sensations.

PROFICIENCY BADGES

Scouts and guides need to qualify for two of the following Proficiency Badges:

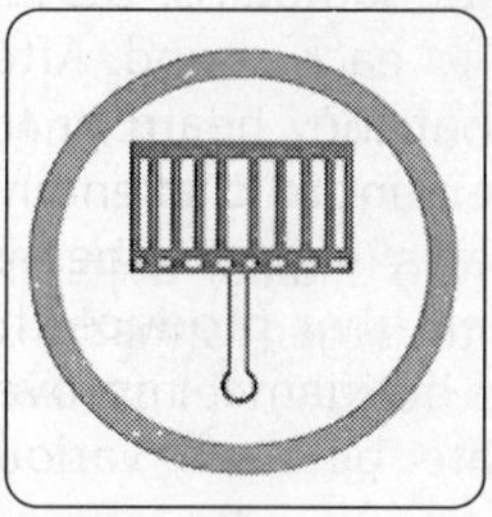

Cook

Debater

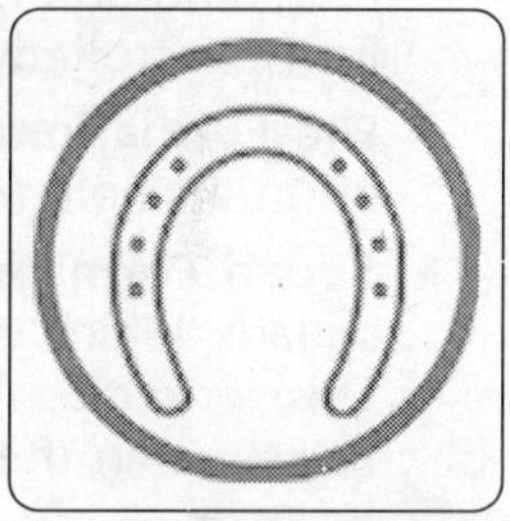

Friend to Animals

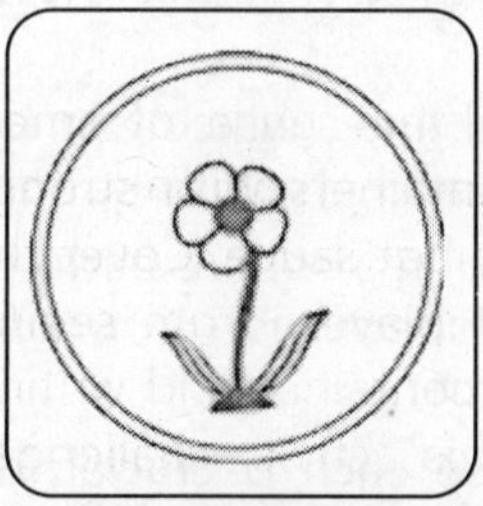

Gardener

Handyman

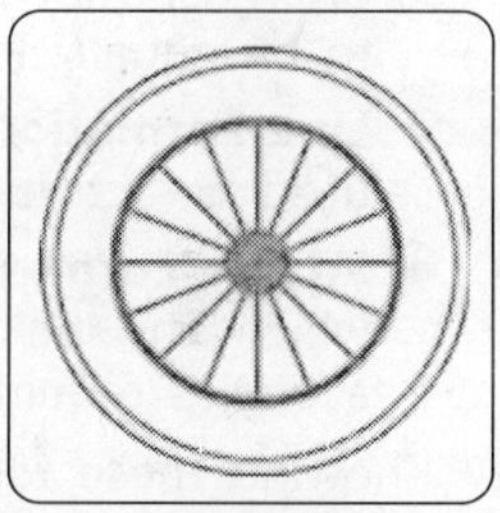

Cyclist

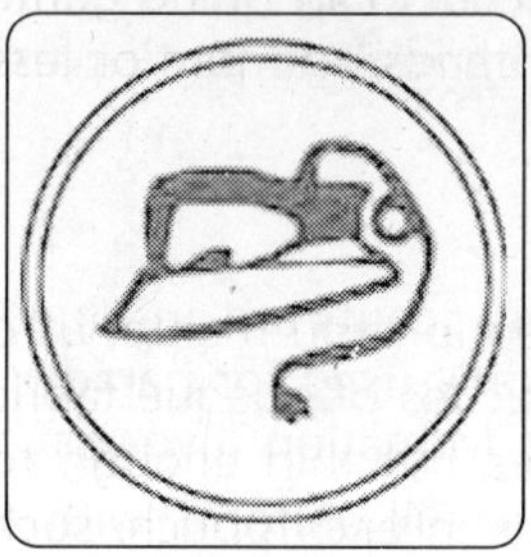

Launder

Reader

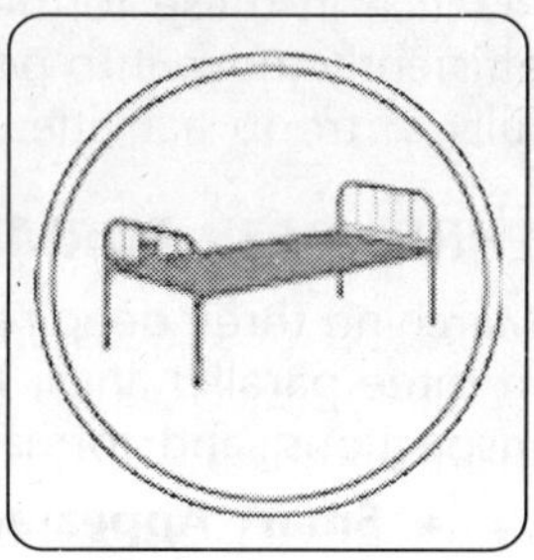

Hospital Man

DISCIPLINE

TROOP FORMATIONS

Understanding troop formations is fundamental to maintaining order and efficiency in scouting activities. Various troop formations are used to organise scouts for different purposes, such as drills, parades, or ceremonies. Common formations include:

- **Column Formation:** Scouts are arranged in a single line, one behind the other. This formation is often used for marching and is useful for moving a large number of scouts in a controlled manner.
- **File Formation:** Similar to the column, but with scouts lined up in a single file, used for orderly movement and assembly.
- **Squad Formation:** Scouts are grouped into smaller units, or squads, which can then be assembled into larger formations. This formation is often used for detailed activities or smaller tasks within the troop.
- **Circle Formation:** Scouts are arranged in a circular pattern, often used for discussions, games, or when all members need to be equally involved.
- **Line Formation:** Scouts stand in parallel lines, which can be used for activities requiring coordination and synchronisation.
- **Square Formation:** Scouts are positioned in a square pattern, which can be used for ceremonies, inspections, or group activities requiring a structured arrangement.

Knowing these formations and when to use each is crucial for effective troop management and the smooth execution of activities. Practice in these formations ensures that all scouts can quickly and efficiently move into position, respond to commands, and participate fully in troop activities.

THREE DEEP FORMATION

Marching three deep refers to a formation where scouts are arranged in three parallel lines. This formation is commonly used for parades, inspections, and formal events. Mastering this formation involves:

- **Smart Appearance:** Scouts should be in full uniform, with a neat and tidy appearance. Each scout must maintain proper posture and follow the rhythm of the march.

- **Coordination:** Marching three deep requires scouts to move in unison, maintaining proper distance between each line and ensuring that everyone is aligned. Coordination is key to achieving a disciplined and orderly march.
- **Following Drill Commands:** Scouts must follow commands given by the leader, such as "forward march," "halt," or "left turn." A clear understanding and execution of these commands are essential for maintaining good order during the march.
- **Practice:** Regular practice helps scouts become familiar with the formation and commands, improving their ability to march smartly and in good order. Practice should include drills to refine movements, spacing, and alignment.

Mastery of marching three deep enhances the troop's appearance during formal events and instills a sense of discipline and teamwork among scouts.

ALL FAITH PRAYER MEETINGS

Scouts are required to participate in four all faith prayer meetings as it is an integral part of fostering inclusivity and respect within the scout troop. These meetings provide a platform for scouts to engage in spiritual reflection and communal activities, transcending individual beliefs. These meetings contribute to the growth and unity of the troop in the following ways:

- **Understanding and Respect:** All-faith prayer meetings are crafted to accommodate the diverse religious backgrounds of scouts. The primary goal is to foster an environment of mutual respect and understanding. Scouts are encouraged to approach these meetings with an open mind, recognising and appreciating the various faith traditions represented. This respectful attitude helps create a harmonious atmosphere where all participants feel valued, regardless of their personal beliefs.
- **Active Participation:** Active participation is crucial in these meetings. Scouts are encouraged to take part in various ways, whether it involves leading prayers, sharing personal reflections, or simply being present and attentive. Engaging actively helps to build a sense of community and promotes mutual respect among scouts. Each scout's involvement contributes to the collective experience, making the meeting more meaningful and impactful.

- **Inclusivity:** Inclusivity is a key feature of all-faith prayer meetings. The aim is to ensure that every scout feels welcomed and valued. Meetings should incorporate elements from various faiths or focus on universal values that resonate with all participants. This approach helps in creating a supportive environment where scouts from different backgrounds can connect and find common ground, enhancing the overall sense of belonging within the troop.
- **Reflection and Learning:** These meetings provide an opportunity for scouts to learn about and reflect on different religious traditions and practices. Engaging with diverse perspectives broadens their understanding and fosters a more inclusive environment. Reflection on different faiths and practices helps scouts appreciate the richness of various traditions, contributing to their personal growth and spiritual development.

PRATAH SMARAN

This is a prayer that reflects on the divine essence and transcendent reality. It is recited in the morning and focuses on the eternal and formless nature of the divine, emphasising the unity of existence beyond the physical and material world.

Pratah smarami hridi sansfuradatma tatvam,
Sat chit sukham paramhansagatim turiyam,
Yat swapna jagar sushuptamavaiti Nityam,
Tad brahma nishkalamaham na cha bhut sanghah...(1)

Pratarbhajami manso vachasamagamyam,
Vacho vibhanti nikhila yadanugrahena,
Yanneti neti vachanair nigamamavochus,
Tam deva deva majamachyuta rahuragryma....(2)

Pratar namami tamaso paramarkavarnam,
Punam sanatana padam purushottamakhyam,
Yasmin idam jagadasheshamashesh murti,
Rajva bhujangmaiva pratibhashitam vai....(3)

SARASWATI VANDANA

This prayer is dedicated to Goddess Saraswati, the deity of knowledge and wisdom. It seeks her blessings for removing ignorance and bestowing knowledge.

Ya kundendu tusharahara dhavala, ya shubhravastravrita,
Ya vina brahmachyutashankaraprabhritibhir devaisadavandita.
Sa mam patu saraswati bhagvati, nihshesh jadya paha.

GURU VANDANA

This prayer acknowledges the importance of the guru (teacher) as a divine figure and the embodiment of knowledge and wisdom.

Gurubrahma guruvishnu gurudevo maheshvarah,
Guru sakshat parabrahma, tasmai shri guravenamah.

RAM DHUN

This devotional chant is dedicated to Lord Rama, invoking his blessings and the universal name of God.

Raghupati Raghav Rajaram
Patita pavan sitaram,
Sita ram, sitaram,
Bhaj pyare tu sitaram .... Raghupati
Ishwar Allah Tere Nam
Sabko sanmati de bhagavan ..... Raghupati

- **Concluding the Prayer Meeting:** At the end of the all-faith prayer meeting, there is a moment of silence to reflect on the experience and connect with the divine. The leader may provide brief instructions if necessary, and then all participants should quietly disperse without talking. This silence emphasises the spiritual significance of the moment, reinforcing the sense of unity with the Almighty.

- **Documentation:** Scouts and Guides should record each prayer meeting in their notebooks. Upon completing four all-faith prayer meetings, they should obtain a signature from the Scoutmaster (S.M.) or Guide Captain (G.C.) to acknowledge their participation. This documentation serves as a record of their commitment to fostering inclusivity and respect within the troop.

COMMUNICATION

ADVANTAGES AND DISADVANTAGES OF COMPUTER, MOBILE PHONES, INTERNET AND THEIR APPLICATION

1. Using a Computer

Advantages

- **Productivity Tools:** Computers provide access to productivity tools such as word processors, spreadsheets, and presentation software, which are essential for creating documents, managing data, and preparing presentations.
- **Internet Access:** Computers allow for efficient browsing, research, and communication via email and social media. They offer a larger screen and a more comfortable typing experience compared to mobile devices.
- **Software Applications:** Many professional software applications, such as graphic design tools, video editing software, and programming environments, are more robust and accessible on computers.
- **Storage and Backup:** Computers typically have more storage capacity for saving files and can be used for backup purposes to secure important data.

Disadvantages

- **Portability:** Computers, especially desktops, are less portable compared to mobile devices, making them less convenient for on-the-go use.
- **Cost:** High-performance computers can be expensive to purchase and maintain.

- **Complexity:** Computers may require more technical knowledge to troubleshoot and maintain compared to simpler devices like mobile phones.

2. Mobile Phones

Advantages

- **Portability:** Mobile phones are highly portable, allowing users to stay connected and access information from almost anywhere.
- **Communication:** They offer various communication options, including voice calls, text messages, email, and social media.
- **Applications:** Mobile phones support a wide range of applications that can assist in productivity, navigation, entertainment, and health.
- **Camera:** Most mobile phones come equipped with high-quality cameras for capturing photos and videos, which can be useful for personal and professional purposes.

Disadvantages

- **Limited Functionality:** Mobile phones have limited functionality compared to computers, especially for complex tasks such as extensive data processing or graphic design.
- **Battery Life:** Mobile phones require regular charging, and their battery life can be a constraint during extended use.
- **Screen Size:** The smaller screen size can be less convenient for detailed work or extended reading.

3. The Internet and Its Applications in the Development of the Country

Advantages

- **Information Access:** The internet provides access to a vast amount of information, facilitating education, research, and awareness. It supports online learning platforms and educational resources.
- **Economic Growth:** E-commerce and online businesses contribute to economic development by providing new opportunities for entrepreneurs and businesses. It also facilitates digital payments and financial inclusion.

- **Government Services:** The internet enables e-governance by making government services more accessible to citizens. Online portals for tax filing, public services, and citizen engagement are examples of this.
- **Healthcare:** Telemedicine and online health resources improve access to healthcare services, particularly in remote areas, and support health education and awareness.

Disadvantages:

- **Digital Divide:** Unequal access to the internet can exacerbate existing social and economic inequalities, leaving some groups disadvantaged.
- **Cybersecurity Risks:** The proliferation of online data increases the risk of cyberattacks, data breaches, and privacy issues.
- **Misinformation:** The spread of false or misleading information on the internet can lead to misinformation and influence public opinion and behaviour negatively.

ACCESSING THE WEBSITES OF THE BHARAT SCOUTS AND GUIDES

Connecting to the Internet

- **Device Setup:** Ensure your device (computer, tablet, or smartphone) is connected to the internet. You can connect via a Wi-Fi network or mobile data.
- **Browser Access:** Open a web browser on your device. This could be Google Chrome, Mozilla Firefox, Safari, or Microsoft Edge.

Navigating the Internet

- **Search Engines:** Use a search engine like Google, Bing, or Yahoo. Enter the keywords "Bharat Scouts and Guides official website" into the search bar and press Enter.
- **Direct URL:** Alternatively, if you know the direct URL, type it into the browser's address bar: https://www.bsgindia.org/ and press Enter.

Navigating the Website

- **Homepage:** When you arrive at the website, you'll be on the homepage. This is where you can find links to various sections, such as Home, Shop, Donate, and Contact Us.
- **Menu and Links:** Use the navigation menu, typically located at the top or side of the page, to explore different sections of the website.

Accessing Specific Information

- **News and Updates:** Look for sections such as 'BSG News' or 'Rules and Regulations' to find the latest updates and announcements.
- **Contact Information:** For further assistance or specific inquiries, visit the 'Contact Us' page. Here, you can find contact details or submit inquiry forms.

By following these steps, you can easily access and navigate the Bharat Scouts and Guides website to find the information and resources you need.

PATRIOTISM

INFORMATION ABOUT HERITAGE AND CULTURE AND PREPARING A LOG:

India, a land of vibrant diversity, offers a unique blend of ancient traditions and modern advancements. Its rich tapestry of heritage includes majestic landscapes, historic monuments, and a profound cultural legacy that spans millennia.

- **A Land of Diversity and Beauty:** India is renowned for its stunning contrasts, from the towering peaks of the Himalayas to the arid expanses of the Thar Desert. This land showcases a vast array of natural beauty, including lush forests, verdant plains, and picturesque river valleys. Each region boasts its own distinct flora and fauna, contributing to a mosaic of ecosystems. The Himalayas, the highest mountain range in the world, present a challenging and awe-inspiring terrain for mountaineers, while the country's numerous wildlife sanctuaries protect species such as tigers, elephants, and exotic birds.

- **Artistic and Architectural Splendour:** India's heritage is marked by its impressive architecture and art. The country is home to numerous ancient monuments and buildings crafted by master artisans. Iconic structures like the Taj Mahal, Qutub Minar, and Red Fort reflect the grandeur of past empires. The intricate carvings and elaborate designs of temples and forts stand testament to India's rich architectural history.
- **Rich Traditions of Craftsmanship:** Indian craftsmanship is celebrated globally for its artistry and skill. In Kashmir, exquisite hand-embroidered shawls are a prized export, while Varanasi and Murshidabad are renowned for their brocades. The jewellery from Delhi and Jaipur, the ivories of Karnataka and Kerala, and the metalware of Moradabad and Hyderabad showcase a range of traditional skills. Each region's craft reflects its cultural heritage and artistic sensibility, contributing to India's reputation as a treasure trove of beautiful artefacts.
- **Theatrical and Dramatic Arts:** Drama in India has ancient roots, with its origins linked to religious rituals and ceremonies. Bharata's Natya Shastra, a classical treatise on dramaturgy, provides insight into early Indian theatrical traditions. Indian drama, characterised by its integration of music, dance, and poetry, emphasises sentiment, or rasa, focusing on the emotional experience of the audience. The tradition of Sanskrit drama is complemented by classical dance forms such as Bharatanatyam, Kathakali, Kathak, Kuchipudi, Odissi, and Manipuri, each representing a unique cultural and artistic heritage.
- **Dance Forms—Classical, Folk, and Tribal:** India's dance traditions are classified into classical, folk, and tribal categories. Classical dances, including Bharatanatyam and Kathak, are performed in urban centres and are characterised by their formal techniques and intricate movements. Folk dances, prevalent in rural areas, celebrate the daily life and agricultural cycles of local communities. Tribal dances, performed by indigenous Adivasi communities, are deeply embedded in their ritualistic practices and reflect their connection to nature and spirituality.

- **The Role of Cinema:** Cinema is a significant cultural phenomenon in India, offering entertainment and a reflection of societal values. The Indian film industry, encompassing Bollywood and regional cinema, produces a diverse array of films. In cities and towns, cinemas are popular venues for both local and international films. The influence of cinema extends beyond entertainment, shaping public opinion and cultural trends.
- **Museums and Historical Sites:** India boasts over two hundred museums that showcase its artistic and archaeological heritage. Museums across the country exhibit artefacts, sculptures, and paintings from various historical periods. Notable sites like Khajuraho, Amaravati, Hampi, and Konark are renowned for their exquisite sculptures and historical significance. These collections provide valuable insights into India's past civilisations and artistic achievements.
- **Festivals and Cultural Celebrations:** Festivals are integral to Indian culture, reflecting the country's diverse religious and cultural practices. Major festivals such as Diwali, Eid, Christmas, and Vaisakhi offer opportunities for communal celebration and personal reflection. Seasonal festivals, often linked to agricultural cycles, feature traditional rituals, artistic expressions, and family gatherings. Rangoli designs and henna patterns are commonly used during festivals, adding a vibrant and artistic touch to the celebrations.

India's heritage and culture present a fascinating and multifaceted picture of a nation that has preserved its ancient traditions while embracing modernity. This blend of old and new, of tradition and innovation, makes India a captivating destination for anyone interested in exploring its rich cultural legacy.

A Dwitiya Sopan Scout/Guide will work for at least six months to qualify for Tritiya Sopan.

CHAPTER

5

TRITIYA SOPAN

Tritiya Sopan is a significant milestone in a Scout's or Guide's journey. At this stage, Scouts and Guides are expected to engage in activities that develop not only their outdoor skills but also their awareness of important social issues. Achieving the Tritiya Sopan signifies a deeper commitment to the principles of Scouting and Guiding, and it opens the way for further advancement.

As part of the requirements for the Tritiya Sopan, Scouts and Guides must deliver a short talk during the Troop meeting on one of the following important topics:

- **National Integration:** Discuss the importance of unity and national identity, highlighting how diverse cultures, traditions, and languages contributes to the strength of the nation.
- **Child Abuser:** Raise awareness about the issue of child abuse, its forms, and the measures to prevent and address it.
- **Substance Abuser:** Educate others on the dangers of substance abuse, the importance of making healthy choices, and how to avoid being influenced by harmful substances.
- **Your Future Scout Training:** Share your vision and goals for your future Scout training, including the skills and knowledge you hope to acquire.
- **Gender Equality:** Talk about the importance of equality between genders and how it contributes to a fair and just society.
- **Child Education, Child Health, Child Social Security & Child Labour:** Address the significance of child welfare, focusing on education, health, and protection against exploitation such as child labour.

- **Free Being Me:** Discuss the value of embracing individuality and respecting the uniqueness of others, fostering an environment of inclusivity and self-expression.

CAMP CRAFT

SAILMAKER'S WHIPPING

Sailmaker's Whipping is a strong way to stop a rope from fraying. It's commonly used for ropes with twisted strands and is especially useful for Scouts and outdoor activities.

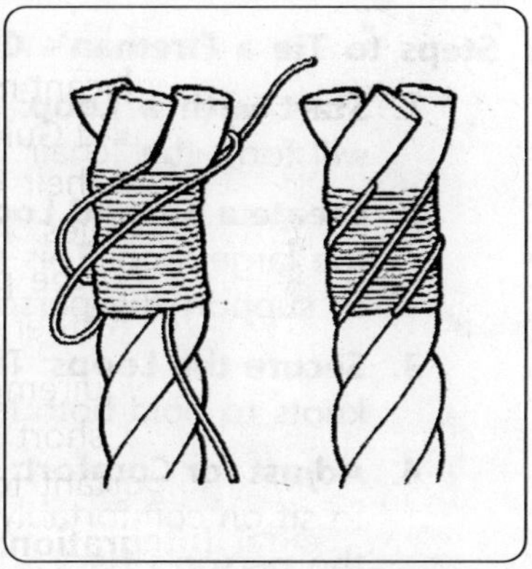

Sailmaker's Whipping

Steps to Do Sailmaker's Whipping:

1. **Get a Needle and Thread:** Use a needle and strong, waxed thread or twine.
2. **Make a Loop:** Thread the needle through the rope about 1 inch from the end to create a small loop.
3. **Wrap the Thread:** Wrap the thread tightly around the rope's end, covering the loop you made. Keep the wraps close together.
4. **Secure the Wrap:** Pass the needle through the wrapped section a few times to hold it firmly.
5. **Trim the Ends:** Cut off any extra thread and rope fibers for a neat finish.

Uses: Sailmaker's whipping is used to prevent the ends of ropes from fraying and to reinforce their strength, ensuring durability and ease of handling. It helps make ropes stronger and easier to use, especially in sailing and outdoor activities. This technique is essential for keeping ropes in good condition, especially when they are exposed to harsh weather or heavy use.

FIREMAN'S CHAIR KNOT

The Fireman's Chair Knot is a specialised knot that forms a secure seat and back support for safely lifting or lowering a person during rescues.

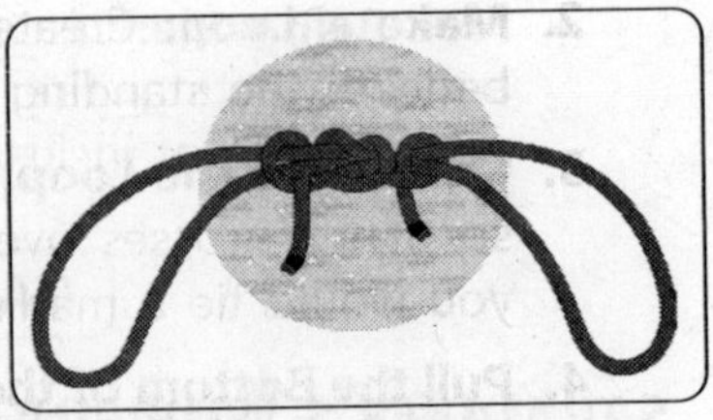

Fireman's Chair Knot

Steps to Tie a Fireman's Chair Knot:

1. **Start with a Loop:** Make a large loop with the rope. This will form the "chair" for sitting.
2. **Create a Second Loop:** Form another smaller loop on top of the large loop. This smaller loop will act as a safety harness to support the person's back.
3. **Secure the Loops:** Tie a basic overhand knot or other secure knots to hold both loops in place, ensuring they do not slip.
4. **Adjust for Comfort:** Make sure the larger loop is wide enough to sit on comfortably and the smaller loop fits snugly around the person's back.
5. **Test the Knot:** Before use, check that the knot is tight and the loops are secure to ensure safety.

Uses: The Fireman's Chair Knot is used in rescue operations to safely lift or lower a person during emergencies like fires or cliff rescues. It creates a secure seat and back support using only rope, ensuring comfort and safety. This knot is essential for firefighters, rescue teams, and adventure training.

MAN HARNESS KNOT

The Man Harness Knot is a secure knot used for tying a rope around a person to ensure safety in rescue situations.

Steps to Tie a Man Harness Knot

Man Harness Knot

1. **Lay the Rope Flat:** Start by laying the rope flat on the ground, with the standing part (the long, fixed section) and the running end (the free, shorter part) visible.

2. **Make a Loop:** Create a loop by bringing the running end beneath the standing part of the rope.
3. **Cross Over the Loop:** Take the running end and pull it down so that it crosses over the top of the loop, similar to how you would tie a marlinspike hitch.
4. **Pull the Bottom of the Loop Through:** Now, pass the bottom of the loop through the gap between the top of the loop and the running end.
5. **Tighten the Knot:** Pull both ends of the rope tightly to secure the knot, making sure the loop fits around the person for safety.

Uses: This knot is primarily used in climbing, rescue operations, and other activities where securing a person with a rope is necessary. It helps distribute weight evenly and ensures that the individual is safely attached to the rope. It is also vital in situations where quick and secure attachment is required.

BOWLINE ON A BITE

The Bowline on a Bite is a strong and secure knot used to form a fixed loop in the middle of a rope.

Steps to Tie a Bowline on a Bite:

1. **Form a Loop:** Start by creating a loop with a bight (a section of rope folded back on itself). Pass the end of the bight over the standing part (the longer section of rope).
2. **Pull Through the Loop:** Pull the bight out through the loop you just created. This is the initial step in forming the knot.
3. **Open the Bight:** Now, open up the bight (the folded section of rope) and bring it around the entire knot. This helps to form the shape of the knot.

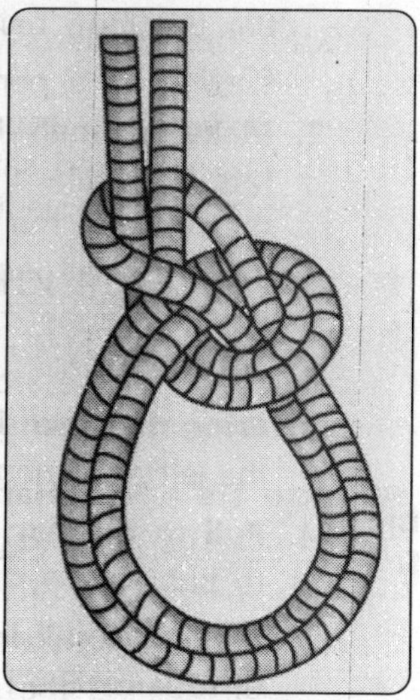

Bowline

4. **Encircle the Standing Ends:** Continue to bring the bight up and over, encircling the standing ends of the rope. The loop will now pass around the standing part.
5. **Tighten the Knot:** Hold the standing part of the rope and pull the loop downwards. This will tighten the knot, securing the loop in place.

Uses: The Bowline on a Bite is often used in climbing, sailing, and rescue operations to create a secure loop for attaching to an anchor or person. It is especially useful when a loop is needed in the middle of a rope without tying the ends together.

DRAW HITCH

The Draw Hitch is an excellent knot for quick-release situations. It can be tied in the middle of a rope, making it useful for hauling or retrieving lines.

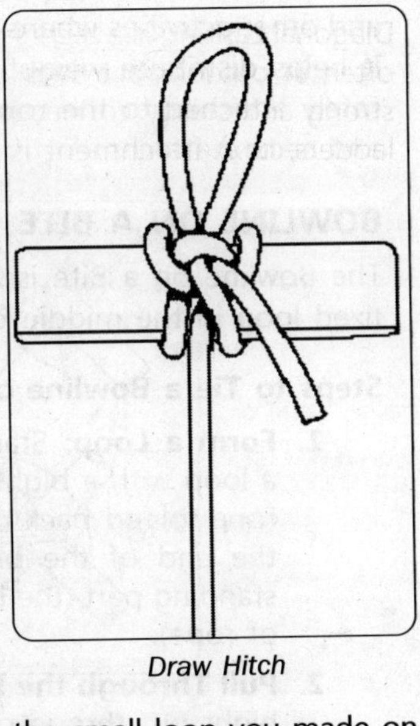

Draw Hitch

Steps to Tie a Draw Hitch:

1. **Make a big loop:** Take part of the rope and make a big loop. Put this loop behind the post or object you want to tie it to.
2. **Make a small loop on the left:** Now, take a small piece of the rope on the left side, and make a small loop with it. Put this loop under the object you are tying it to.
3. **Bring the small loop over:** Take the small loop you made on the left and bring it over the big loop in front.
4. **Pull to tighten:** Pull the small loop up and the rope down to tighten the knot.
5. **Make a small loop on the right:** Now, take a small piece of rope on the right side, and make another small loop. Put this loop under the object, just like you did on the left side.

6. **Put the right loop through the left one:** Take the small loop on the right side and put it through the loop on the left side.
7. **Pull to tighten again:** Pull the right loop up and the left loop down to tighten the knot.

The Draw·Hitch is commonly used for securing a boat to a mooring or a horse to a hitching post, providing a quick-release option when needed. It can also be tied in the middle of a rope to create two equal ends, useful for hauling or lifting tasks.

To Release the Knot: If you want to undo the knot, just pull on the right side, and the knot will come undone easily.

DIAGONAL LASHING

Diagonal Lashing is a technique used to join two poles or sticks together, often in outdoor activities like scouting or construction. It provides a strong and sturdy connection, ideal for building structures like frames, ladders, or A-frames.

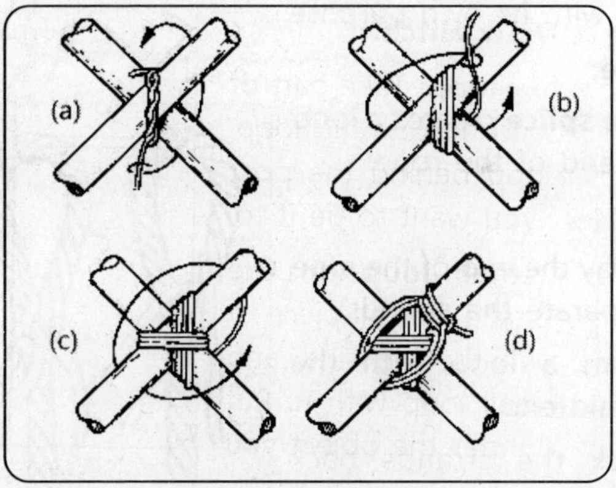

Diagonal Lashing

Steps for Diagonal Lashing:

1. **Position the Poles:** Place the two poles so that they cross each other at an angle, usually about 45 degrees.
2. **Wrap the Rope:** Start by wrapping the rope around the poles where they cross, creating an "X" shape. Pass the rope around the poles several times, keeping the wraps tight.

3. **Make a Diagonal Figure:** After a few wraps, run the rope diagonally over one pole and under the other. This creates the diagonal pattern that strengthens the lashing.
4. **Tighten the Lashing:** Pull the rope tightly to secure the poles in place. You can add more wraps to ensure a strong hold.
5. **Tie Off the End:** Finish by tying off the rope with a secure knot, such as a square knot, to hold everything in place.

Uses: Diagonal lashing is used to join two poles or sticks at an angle, creating a strong, stable connection. It's commonly used in scouting to build structures like frames, ladders, or shelters. The technique is reliable for securing poles in outdoor activities or emergencies, providing a durable and supportive join.

SPLICING - EYE, BACK, AND SHORT

Splicing is a technique used to join the ends of ropes or lines together by interweaving the strands of the rope. There are several types of splicing, each with its own purpose.

1. **Eye Splice:**
   - The **eye splice** creates a loop at the end of the rope.
   - **Steps:**
     1. Unlay the end of the rope (separate the strands).
     2. Form a loop with the unlaid end.
     3. Tuck the strands back into the rope, following the pattern of the strands, until the loop is secure.
     4. Tighten the splice by pulling the strands through and smoothing them out.

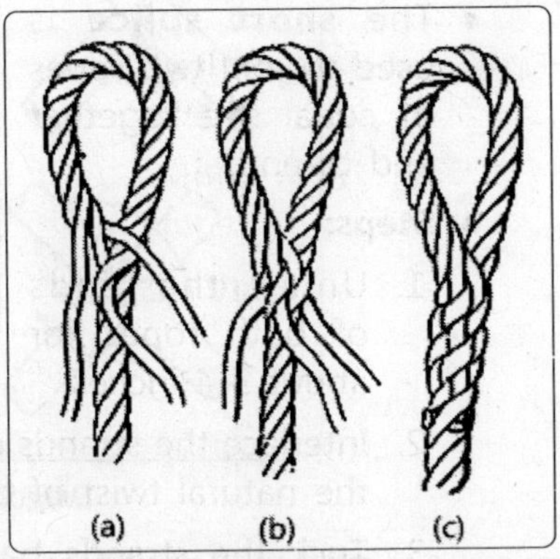

Eye-Splice

   - **Use:** Used for attaching a rope to a ring or creating a permanent loop in the rope, often used in mooring lines or for tying objects securely.

2. Back Splice:

- The **back splice** is used to finish off the end of a rope to prevent it from fraying.
- **Steps:**
  1. Unlay the rope strands for about 3-4 inches.
  2. Twist each strand into a rope and then bind them back onto the rope, wrapping them in the reverse direction.
  3. Continue until the splice is about 4 inches long, ensuring it is tightly wound.
  4. Tuck in the loose ends and trim off any excess.
- **Use:** Primarily used for securing the ends of ropes to prevent fraying, especially for ropes used in climbing or boating.

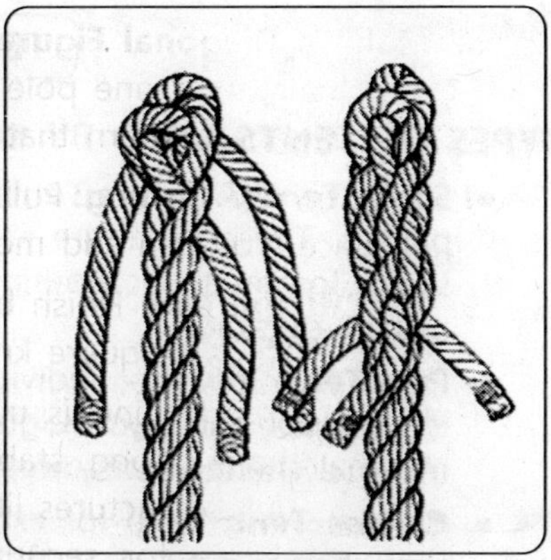

Back Splice

3. Short Splice:

- The **short splice** is used to join two ropes of equal size together end-to-end.
- **Steps:**
  1. Unlay the ends of both ropes for about 3-4 inches.
  2. Interlace the strands of one rope with the other, following the natural twist of the rope.
  3. Tuck the strands back into the body of the rope and continue until the splice is secure.
  4. Tighten the splice and trim any loose ends.
- **Use:** Used to join two ropes together to form a longer length of rope, useful in boating or climbing situations where you need to extend the rope.

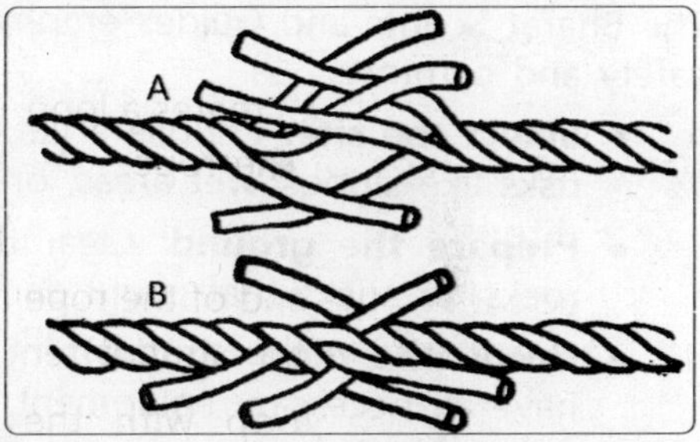

Short Splice

TENT

TYPES OF TENTS USED BY SCOUTS

- **Scout Tent (A-frame Tent):** A common choice for groups and patrols. These tents are simple, strong, and provide enough space for multiple Scouts. They are easy to set up and are usually durable.
- **Pup Tent:** Ideal for individual Scouts or a pair of Scouts. It is compact and lightweight, perfect for short stays or when minimal shelter is required.
- **Canvas Tent:** Used for extended stays in the field. It's made from heavy-duty material that provides extra durability and protection against the elements.
- **Dome Tent:** Less common in some Scout camps, but a good alternative for small groups or individuals looking for a quick setup. They are stable and offer better wind resistance.

TENT PITCHING

The Bharat Scouts and Guides emphasise proper pitching to ensure safety and comfort:

- **Select the site:** Choose a flat, dry area, avoiding places with risks like slopes, wet areas, or spots prone to flooding.
- **Prepare the ground:** Clear the area of any sharp objects, rocks, or sticks that could damage the tent floor.
- **Unroll the tent:** Lay the tent body flat and check that you have all necessary equipment, including poles and ropes.
- **Assemble the poles:** Connect the tent poles carefully, ensuring they are properly fitted into the metal eyelet or pole sleeves on the tent body.
- **Attach the poles to the tent body:** Insert the pole ends into the tent's eyelets, then position the tent structure by raising the poles and allowing the tent to assume its shape.
- **Peg the tent securely:** Start with the four corners and secure the tent with pegs to the ground, ensuring the tent is taut.
- **Adjust the guy ropes:** Once the tent is up, use the guy ropes to further secure the structure. Attach them to the tent's loops or rings and stake them into the ground at an angle.

STRIKING THE TENT

- **Remove the pegs and guy ropes:** Untie the guy ropes and remove the pegs, ensuring they are kept together and stored correctly for the next use.
- **Disassemble the poles:** Carefully take down the poles, making sure not to damage or bend them.
- **Clean the tent:** Shake the tent to remove debris, dirt, or dust, and wipe off any excess moisture before folding it.
- **Fold the tent carefully:** Fold the tent in a way that avoids creases and helps it fit into its storage bag properly.
- **Store the tent dry:** If the tent is wet, spread it out to dry before packing it away to prevent mold or mildew growth.

IMPROVING TENT SETUP

The Bharat Scouts and Guides encourage improving the quality of your tent setup by focusing on durability, comfort, and safety:

- **Use a Groundsheet:** Place a groundsheet beneath the tent to protect the floor from wear and keep moisture out.
- **Ensure Good Ventilation:** Open any vents or windows to allow airflow, which will reduce condensation and keep the inside of the tent dry and fresh.
- **Waterproof the Tent:** Treat the tent with waterproofing solutions regularly, particularly on seams, zippers, and the rainfly to ensure the tent remains water-resistant in wet conditions.
- **Check the Tent Regularly:** Inspect the tent for wear and tear, particularly the seams, zippers, and pole structure, and make repairs as needed.
- **Use the Rainfly:** Always use the rainfly to ensure the tent is protected from rain and adverse weather conditions. It provides an additional layer of protection.
- **Secure the Tent Properly:** Tighten the guy ropes and pegs securely to withstand winds. Ensure the tent remains taut and stable to avoid damage in adverse weather.

ADDITIONAL TIPS FOR SCOUTS

- **Respect the Environment:** Scouts are encouraged to use Leave No Trace principles. This means cleaning up the camp area, ensuring no waste is left behind, and keeping the surrounding nature intact.
- **Teamwork in Pitching Tents:** Tent pitching often involves teamwork. Scouts learn valuable cooperation skills by working together to set up, maintain, and strike tents.
- **Learning Outdoor Skills:** These activities not only teach tent management but also valuable life skills such as responsibility, planning, and attention to detail.

PIONEERING

MAKING A FLAG MAST OF AT LEAST THREE STAVES

Making a Flag Mast of at Least Three Staves is a skill that Scouts can learn as part of their outdoor activities. It involves constructing a mast that is sturdy and can support a flag for events or ceremonies. This task encourages teamwork, planning, and the practical application of construction techniques.

Steps for Making the Flag Mast:

1. **Prepare the Staves**
   - Cut the three wooden staves to a similar length (depending on how high you want your mast to be). A typical height for a flag mast is about 10-15 feet.
   - Ensure that the staves are straight and free from splinters. Sand them down if necessary to ensure smoothness.
2. **Position the Staves**
   - Lay the three staves on the ground, parallel to each other. Arrange them so that they are spaced evenly apart.
   - Decide the formation you want for your mast. For added strength, place two of the staves vertically, and the third can be placed horizontally to brace the structure.

3. **Drill Holes for Support**
   - Drill small holes near the tops and bottoms of the staves where they will be joined.
   - The holes should be large enough to allow the ropes or nails to go through but small enough to create a secure hold.
4. **Join the Staves Together**
   - Using nails, screws, or thick rope, join the three staves together. If using rope, tie them tightly at the junctions.
   - Ensure that the mast remains straight and the staves are tightly secured to prevent wobbling.
5. **Secure with Cross Braces (Optional)**
   - If you want extra stability, you can add cross braces. These are diagonal pieces of wood or rope that connect the three staves in the shape of a "X" for more support.
   - Attach the braces securely with nails or rope, ensuring they are tight.
6. **Final Check**
   - Stand the mast up and check its stability. Make sure it stands upright and is firmly anchored. If necessary, add additional ropes or pegs at the bottom to prevent it from tipping over.
   - Ensure there is enough height for your flag to fly freely without obstruction.

SWIMMING

SAFETY RULES OF SWIMMING

Safety in swimming is crucial, especially for Scouts, as it ensures their well-being while engaging in water activities.

1. **Never Swim Alone**
   - Always swim with a buddy or in a group. Never swim alone, as someone needs to be present to assist in case of an emergency.

2. **Obey the Rules**
   - Follow all the safety rules set by the swimming pool or water body. Adhere to the instructions of lifeguards and other supervisors.
   - Always swim in designated areas where lifeguards are present.
3. **Check the Water Conditions**
   - Ensure the water is clean and safe before swimming. Avoid swimming in dirty or polluted water.
   - Check the weather and water conditions (waves, currents) to ensure they are suitable for swimming.
4. **Warm-Up and Cool-Down**
   - Before swimming, always warm up your body by doing light exercises. Similarly, after swimming, cool down to prevent muscle strains or cramps.
5. **Never Push or Shove**
   - Avoid pushing, shoving, or jumping onto others in the pool or water to prevent accidents or injuries.
6. **Supervision**
   - Always ensure an adult or a qualified lifeguard supervises swimmers, especially when swimming in open water or unfamiliar places.
7. **Use of Swimming Equipment**
   - If using swimming aids (like life jackets or floaters), ensure they are properly fitted and in good condition.
   - Avoid using flotation devices in deep waters or if you are not comfortable in swimming.
8. **Avoid Swimming Immediately After Eating**
   - Wait at least 30 minutes to an hour after eating before swimming to avoid cramps or discomfort in the water.
9. **Know Your Limits**
   - Swim within your skill level and never venture into deep water if you are not comfortable. Do not engage in risky behaviors like diving in unfamiliar areas.

10. **Avoid Swimming Under the Influence**
   - Never swim if you are tired, sick, or have consumed alcohol or drugs. It can impair your judgment and coordination, increasing the risk of accidents.
11. **Use Proper Swimming Attire**
   - Wear proper swimming attire such as swim trunks or swimsuits that allow free movement. Avoid wearing clothing that may restrict movement or cause drag in the water.
12. **Learn Basic Life-Saving Skills**
   - Scouts should learn basic life-saving skills, including CPR and first aid, to assist others in case of an emergency.
13. **Safe Entry and Exit**
   - When entering or exiting the water, use the proper steps, ladders, or other safe methods. Avoid jumping or diving in shallow water.
14. **Avoid Swimming in Dangerous Areas**
   - Do not swim in areas where there are strong currents, near rocks, or where it is not safe to enter the water. Always check for signs that indicate whether swimming is permitted.

DEALING WITH CRAMPS

Dealing with cramps, especially while swimming or engaging in outdoor activities, is essential for maintaining safety and comfort. Here's how to handle cramps:

1. **Recognise the Symptoms of a Cramp**
   - A cramp is a sudden, painful contraction of a muscle. It usually occurs in the legs (calf muscles, hamstrings) but can affect any muscle.
   - The affected area may feel tight, hard, and sore.
2. **Stay Calm**
   - If you experience a cramp while swimming or during any other physical activity, remain calm. Panicking can make the situation worse.

3. **Stop Moving**
   - If you are swimming, stop immediately and try to float or move to a safe area.
   - If you are walking or engaging in other activities, stop the movement and rest the affected muscle.
4. **Stretch and Massage**
   - **For leg cramps:** Straighten your leg and gently pull your toes towards your body. This helps stretch the cramped muscle. If it's a calf cramp, you can pull the top of your foot toward your shin.
   - **Massage:** Gently massage the cramping muscle with your hands to help it relax.
5. **Apply Heat or Cold**
   - **Heat:** Use a warm compress or a heating pad to relax the muscle after the cramp subsides.
   - **Cold:** If the muscle remains sore, apply a cold compress or ice pack wrapped in a cloth to reduce inflammation.
6. **Hydrate**
   - Dehydration is a common cause of muscle cramps. Drink plenty of water, especially after physical activity, to keep your body hydrated.
   - Electrolyte-rich drinks (containing sodium, potassium, and magnesium) can help replenish lost minerals, which may reduce cramping.
7. **Reposition Yourself**
   - If you're swimming and get a cramp, you can gently change your body position. For example, in case of a leg cramp, floating on your back with your legs relaxed can help ease the discomfort.
8. **Rest and Recover**
   - Once the cramp subsides, give your muscles a little rest before continuing any activity. Avoid sudden movements and allow the muscle to fully recover.

9. Prevention for the Future

- **Stretching:** Always stretch before and after physical activities to keep your muscles flexible.
- **Hydration:** Regularly drink water and consume foods rich in potassium, magnesium, and calcium.
- **Warm-Up:** A proper warm-up before strenuous activities can help prevent cramps.

ESTIMATION

HEIGHT UPTO 30 METERS

There are several methods for estimating the height of an object or structure, such as a tree or a tower. These methods can be used when no measuring instruments are available, relying instead on indirect techniques.

1. **Twelve to One Method:** This method is used to estimate the height of an object when you can measure its shadow.

   Steps:

   - Stand at a known distance from the object (e.g., 12 meters).
   - Measure the length of the shadow cast by the object.
   - If the length of the shadow is 1 meter, the height of the object is 12 meters. If the shadow is longer, multiply the distance by the ratio (12:1) to estimate the height.
   - For example, if the shadow is 2 meters, the height of the object is approximately 24 meters (2 meters × 12).

2. **Lumberman's Method:** This is another practical method that uses a stick or straight object.

   Steps:

   - Hold a stick or any straight object of known length upright, and position it so that it casts a shadow at the same time as the object whose height you want to estimate.
   - Measure the length of the stick's shadow.

- Now, compare the ratio of the object's shadow to the stick's shadow. This gives a rough estimate of the height.
- If the stick's height and shadow length are known, you can use a proportion to estimate the height of the object.

3. **Shadow Method:** This method relies on the principle that the ratio of an object's height to its shadow remains constant at a given time of day.

   Steps:

   - Measure the length of the shadow cast by the object.
   - Measure the shadow of a known object, like a stick of known height.
   - Using the proportion (height of known object / length of its shadow) = (height of the object / length of its shadow), calculate the height of the object.

4. **Red Indian Method:** This method uses basic trigonometry and a technique where you estimate the height of an object by comparing it to an object of known size (like a tree or another reference object).

   Steps:

   - Stand at a known distance from the object.
   - Use your thumb or hand to estimate how many times the height of the object fits into the object in view.
   - Multiply the number of estimations by the size of the reference object to estimate the height.

DEPTH UPTO 30 METERS

To estimate the depth of a water body (like a well or a river), there are several methods you can use.

1. **Using a Plumb Line:** A plumb line is a simple method to estimate depth.

   Steps:

   - Drop a weighted object (stone or any suitable weight) tied to a string into the water.

- Let it sink to the bottom, then measure the length of the string to get an estimate of the depth.

2. **Sounding Method:** This involves using a long rope or cord with a weight tied to the end.

Steps:

- Lower the weighted rope into the water until it touches the bottom.
- Pull the rope back up and measure the length of the rope to determine the depth.

WEIGHT UPTO 8 KILOGRAMS

This method is used when you need to estimate the weight of an object without scales.

1. **Balance or Lever Method:**

Steps:

- Use a known weight (such as a bag of 1 kg) as a reference.
- Place the unknown object on one side of a makeshift balance (like a board or stick).
- Place the known weight on the other side until the board or stick is balanced.
- Adjust the known weight until the balance is even, then calculate the total weight of the object by multiplying the number of reference weights by their value.

2. **Comparative Method:**

Steps:

- Compare the object to a known weight by lifting them both in your hands.
- Estimate the weight based on how they feel in comparison to each other. This method is not very precise but can give a rough estimate for objects of similar size and material.

FIRST AID

DROWNING

Drowning is when someone cannot breathe due to their airway being submerged in water. It can be caused by accidents in swimming pools, lakes, or even in shallow water. The victim may initially struggle, but as the situation worsens, they may become unconscious.

First Aid for Drowning:

1. **Rescue the victim:** Quickly remove the person from the water. Ensure your own safety first by avoiding putting yourself at risk.
2. **Check for breathing:** If the person is not breathing, perform rescue breathing (mouth-to-mouth or mouth-to-nose resuscitation).
3. **Start CPR:** If there is no pulse, begin CPR (Cardiopulmonary Resuscitation).
4. **Monitor the person:** Keep the person warm and seek emergency medical help to ensure there are no complications, such as secondary drowning, which can occur after being rescued.

ELECTRIC SHOCK

Electric Shock happens when a person comes into contact with an electric current. It can cause serious injuries such as burns, heart failure, and respiratory issues.

First Aid for Electric Shock:

1. **Turn off the power source:** If possible, switch off the electricity or remove the victim from the source using a non-conductive object like a wooden stick or rubber gloves.
2. **Check the victim's pulse and breathing:** If the person is not breathing, start rescue breathing immediately.
3. **If no pulse:** Perform CPR (Cardiopulmonary Resuscitation).
4. **Seek medical help:** Even if the person seems to recover, it is important to call for medical assistance as there can be internal injuries or delayed symptoms.

GENERAL SHOCK

Shock is a medical emergency where the body's organs and tissues don't receive enough blood flow. It can be caused by severe blood loss, dehydration, burns, or other trauma.

Symptoms of Shock:

1. Feeling cold
2. Sweating
3. Difficulty in breathing
4. Thirst
5. Paleness of lips and face
6. Cold and moist skin
7. Rapid and weak pulse
8. Dry tongue
9. Short, rapid breathing
10. Unconsciousness (if severe)

Treatment of Shock:

1. **Check consciousness:** Determine if the person is conscious and if they can respond.
2. **Find out the cause:** Identify if the shock is due to blood loss, trauma, or other causes.
3. **Position the person properly:** Place the casualty flat on their back, with their head slightly lower than the legs to improve blood circulation to vital organs.
4. **Turn to one side if vomiting:** If the person vomits, turn them on their side to prevent choking.
5. **Loosen tight clothing:** Remove any tight or restrictive clothing to improve circulation.
6. **Keep warm:** Cover the person with a blanket or sheet to prevent further heat loss.
7. **Offer water or ice:** If the person is conscious, give sips of water or cracked ice.
8. **Medical help:** Transport the person to the hospital immediately.

AUTOMOBILE ACCIDENTS

In automobile accidents, injuries are usually caused by the impact, leading to fractures, lacerations, or internal injuries.

First Aid for Automobile Accidents:

1. **Ensure safety:** Move the person from danger if necessary, but do not move them if there are suspected spinal injuries.
2. **Check for injuries:** Examine the casualty for visible injuries such as bleeding, fractures, or head injuries.
3. **Control bleeding:** Apply pressure on wounds to control bleeding.
4. **Immobilise fractures:** Use splints or makeshift materials to stabilise fractures.
5. **Call for medical help:** Always seek professional medical assistance for accident victims, even if injuries appear minor.

HUMAN BEING CAUGHT IN FIRE

Recognising Burns: A burn can be from direct flame contact, hot surfaces, or chemicals. The severity of the burn can vary from first-degree (minor redness) to third-degree (deep tissue damage).

First Aid for Burns and Fire Victims:

1. **Stop, Drop, and Roll:** If the person is on fire, instruct them to stop moving, drop to the ground, and roll to extinguish the flames.
2. **Cool the burn:** Place the burn under cold running water for at least 10 minutes.
3. **Cover the burn:** Cover the burn with a clean, non-stick cloth or sterile dressing to prevent infection.
4. **Do not remove stuck clothing:** If clothing is stuck to the burn, leave it and seek medical help immediately.

CHOKING

Choking occurs when a foreign object blocks the airway, making it difficult for the victim to breathe, speak, or cough. The face may turn bluish and the person may collapse.

First Aid for Choking:

1. **Back Blows:** Administer 5 back blows between the shoulder blades using the heel of your hand.
2. **Finger Sweep:** If the object is visible, use your finger to remove it from the mouth.
3. **Heimlich Maneuver:** Stand behind the casualty, place your arms around their waist, and perform inward and upward thrusts (in the diaphragm area). This will help expel the object from the airway.

FRACTURES (COLLAR BONE, UPPER ARM, FOREARM, HIP, LOWER LEG)

A fracture is the break or crack in a bone, which can happen due to falls, accidents, or high-impact trauma. A fractured bone may lead to pain, swelling, bruising, and an inability to move or use the affected body part. It's important to properly manage fractures to prevent further injury and complications.

Signs of a Fracture:

1. **Deformity (D):** The injured area may appear misaligned, bent, or deformed. In some cases, the bone may protrude from the skin.
2. **Unnatural Mobility (U):** The injured limb may move in ways it shouldn't, due to the dislocation or break in the bone.
3. **Crepitus (C):** A crackling or crunching sound may be heard or felt when the fractured area is moved. This occurs due to the bone ends rubbing together.

General Management of Fractures:

1. **Do not attempt to straighten the limb:** Trying to realign the bone could cause more damage. It is best to leave the limb in the position it is found in.
2. **Cover any open wounds with sterile dressings:** If the bone has pierced the skin, it is important to cover the wound with sterile material. Do not apply pressure directly over the broken bone.

3. **No need for elaborate dressings:** You don't need to apply complicated bandages or dressings. Just ensure that the fracture is stable and immobilized.
4. **Use padding:** Fill in any natural hollows around the injury (such as the armpit or knee) with soft padding (cloth, towel, or any soft material) to prevent further movement.
5. **Immobilize above and below the joint:** Stabilize both the part of the limb above and below the fracture to prevent the bone from moving.
6. **Immobilize the injured part to the body:** For fractures in the arms, tie the arm to the body to reduce the movement. For leg fractures, tie the legs together to prevent movement.
7. **Avoid rigid splints:** It is important not to use rigid splints that may cause more harm. Instead, use flexible materials like cloth or bandages.
8. **Padding before bandaging:** Always add padding (cloth or soft material) to the area before wrapping it with a bandage. This provides additional comfort and protection.
9. **Treat for shock:** Always check for signs of shock (pale face, rapid breathing, weakness). Keep the patient warm, lie them down, and raise their legs if possible.
10. **Arrange for hospital transfer:** Fractures require medical attention. Arrange to get the patient to a hospital or medical professional as soon as possible for proper treatment.

Specific Management for Fractures:

1. **Fracture of the Arm:**
    - Flex the elbow slowly and gently, bringing the forearm against the chest to reduce movement.
    - Tie a collar and cuff sling to support the arm and prevent further stress on the injury.
    - Use a transverse bandage around the chest, fixing the arm against the body. This helps prevent the arm from moving and ensures stability.

2. **Fracture of the Leg:**
   - **Padding:** Fill all natural hollows around the injury, such as the knee or ankle, to prevent movement.
   - **Align the other leg with the fractured leg:** This helps in stabilizing the injured limb.
   - Tie both ankles together with a figure-eight bandage to keep them in position.
   - Tie the knees together to reduce leg movement.
   - Use broad bandages above and below the fracture to secure the fracture and keep the leg immobilized.
   - If both legs are fractured, use two long padded splints to secure both feet. These splints should be padded well to prevent further injury and should be tied to the body with bandages.

HEAT STROKE AND SUN STROKE

Heat Stroke is caused by prolonged exposure to high temperatures and dehydration. Sun Stroke is a related condition caused by excessive exposure to direct sunlight.

First Aid for Heat Stroke and Sun Stroke:

1. **Move the person to a cooler area:** Get them out of direct sunlight and into a shaded area.
2. **Cool the body:** Use cool water or wet towels to bring down the person's temperature. Avoid ice water, as it can cause shock.
3. **Hydrate:** Give small sips of water if the person is conscious.
4. **Seek medical help:** Heat stroke is a medical emergency; immediate professional treatment is necessary.

RESCUE BREATHING AND CPR (CARDIO PULMONARY RESUSCITATION)

Rescue Breathing is used when the casualty is not breathing but has a pulse.

Steps for Rescue Breathing:

1. **Position the casualty:** Lay the person flat on their back.
2. **Clear the airway:** Open the mouth and clear any visible obstructions.
3. **Mouth-to-mouth or Mouth-to-Nose:** Seal your mouth over theirs and exhale air into their lungs, watching for chest rise.
4. **Continue rescue breaths:** Give 5 rapid breaths and then 8-12 breaths per minute, maintaining the rhythm for an hour or until the casualty begins to breathe independently.

CPR is used when the heart has stopped beating. It combines chest compressions and rescue breathing to circulate blood and oxygen to vital organs.

Steps for CPR:

1. **Check for pulse:** Ensure there is no pulse.
2. **Chest compressions:** Place your hands in the center of the chest, and press down firmly at a rate of 100-120 compressions per minute.
3. **Rescue breaths:** After 30 compressions, give 2 rescue breaths. Continue the cycle of compressions and breaths until help arrives.

RECOVERY POSITION

The recovery position helps maintain an open airway in an unconscious person who is breathing.

1. **Lay the person on their side.**
2. **Tilt their head** back to keep the airway open.
3. **Bend the top leg** so the knee is at a right angle.
4. **Place the bottom arm** under the head for support.

TRANSPORTATION OF A VICTIM

If the victim needs to be moved, it's essential to do so safely to prevent further injury.

1. **Do not move the victim unless necessary.**
2. **Use a stretcher:** If available, use a stretcher to move the victim.
3. **Improvised carry:** If no stretcher is available, use a cloth or blanket to support the person.
4. **Transport with care:** Ensure that the victim remains as stable as possible while being moved.

MAPPING

TRIANGULATION METHOD

The triangulation method is a technique used in surveying and map-making to determine the positions of various points on the ground by forming triangles.

Steps for Drawing a Map Using the Triangulation Method:

1. **Choose Two Known Points:** Select two points that are visible from a location where you can observe both points clearly. These points should be well-marked and easily identifiable on the ground, such as a building, a tree, or a landmark. These points are called station points or reference points.
2. **Measure the Distance Between the Two Points:** If possible, measure the distance between the two known points (referred to as base line). This distance will form the base of your triangle and is important for creating a scale for your map. In practical cases, this might not always be possible, but an estimate of the distance will work for drawing a basic map.
3. **Set Up a Protractor or Theodolite:** Use a protractor or a simple theodolite (or even a compass) to measure the angles from each of the known points towards the unknown points. The unknown points are those locations you want to mark on the map but do not have exact coordinates for. Record these angles accurately for precise results.
4. **Take Measurements at Different Locations:** Move to the unknown location (for which you want to create the map) and measure the angles between the line of sight and the two known reference points. It's important to measure the angles carefully to ensure accuracy.

5. **Draw the Triangular Shape:** On a piece of paper, draw a line between the two reference points. This line will serve as the base of your triangle. Using the recorded angles, plot the directions towards the unknown point (or points) from each reference point. The intersection of these lines will give the location of the unknown point.
6. **Create the Map:**
   - Draw a simple representation of the area using a scale (e.g., 1 cm = 10 m or 1 cm = 100 m). You can use the distances between points to scale them correctly on the paper.
   - Label each point, including the reference points and any additional landmarks or features you can identify.
   - You can also mark the compass directions (North, South, East, West) to give context to the map.
7. **Plot Additional Points:** If needed, repeat the triangulation method from different locations or using different angles to add more points to your map. Continue using the same method of measuring angles and plotting the intersections to refine your map.

ROAD TRAVERSE METHOD or GILWELL SKETCH

The Road Traverse Method, also known as the Gilwell Sketch, is a simple yet effective way for scouts to sketch maps of an area by following a specific route, or road, and recording observations along the way. This method is typically used for creating rough maps of areas where detailed surveys are not necessary, and it is ideal for navigation or tracking a route.

Steps for Sketching a Map Using the Road Traverse Method:

1. **Preparation:**
   - **Select the area to map:** Choose a small section of the area you will be exploring. This could be a trail, a path, or a section of a campsite.

- **Gather materials:** You'll need a notebook, pencil, ruler, compass (optional), and possibly a measuring device (like a pace counter or measuring wheel) to estimate distances.

2. **Start from a Known Reference Point:**
   - Choose a known point in the area where you begin the traverse (e.g., a landmark, the starting point of a trail, or a campsite).
   - Mark this point on your map, or note it in your notes as the starting point.

3. **Mark the Road or Path:**

   As you walk along the road or path, take note of key features along the route, such as:
   - Turns (left or right)
   - Junctions with other paths or roads
   - Landmarks (buildings, trees, rocks, water sources, etc.)
   - Changes in terrain (e.g., from flat ground to a slope or hill)

   Measure or estimate the distance between features (if possible, using pacing or a measuring device). You may not need exact measurements; rough estimates are sufficient for this method.

4. **Record Details as You Move Along:**

   As you proceed, make note of the following:
   - Directions of turns (use a compass for accuracy or note turns based on your sense of direction).
   - The type of terrain or surface (e.g., paved road, dirt track, grassy area, rocky).
   - Distances between major landmarks or turns. If you're unable to measure the distance exactly, estimate using paces.
   - Other observations like nearby buildings, rivers, bridges, or important features that help define the route.

5. **Draw the Sketch:**

   Using the recorded notes, begin sketching the route on your paper or map.

   - **Use a simple scale:** While the Gilwell Sketch doesn't need to be perfectly to scale, make sure your map is proportional. You can represent distances roughly in a proportion that fits the area you're sketching.
   - Draw the path as it winds through the terrain, marking the features as you have recorded them.
   - **Include relevant features:** Place the junctions, landmarks, and changes in terrain on the map to create a visual guide.

6. **Review and Finalise the Sketch:**

   - Once you've sketched the entire route, go back over your notes and ensure that all important features are included.
   - Label all the major landmarks or features that are essential to understanding the route.
   - Make sure the route is clear, and any directions or distances are noted properly, so that someone else can follow it based on your sketch.

7. **Optional – Add a Compass Rose:**

   - If you've recorded directions along the route, you can add a compass rose to show the orientation (e.g., North, South, East, West).
   - This will make it easier to follow the directions on your map.

8. **Use a Key or Legend:**

   Add a simple key or legend to the map to explain any symbols or shorthand you've used. For example:

   - A solid line for a main road
   - A dotted line for a side path
   - Squares for buildings
   - Triangles for trees or hills

OUTDOOR ACTIVITIES

PLANNING AN OVERNIGHT PATROL CAMP

Objective: An overnight patrol camp offers an opportunity for scouts to practice various camping skills, including setting up tents, cooking, teamwork, and navigation. It allows scouts to experience outdoor living, learn survival skills, and foster cooperation.

- **Choose a Safe Location:** Pick a campsite that is suitable and safe for the patrol.
- **Prepare Equipment:** Pack essentials like tents, food, water, and first aid kits.
- **Assign Roles:** Each patrol member gets a task (like cooking, setting up tents, etc.).
- **Camp Activities:** Plan activities such as hiking, games, and campfire storytelling.
- **Clean Up:** After the camp, clean the campsite and pack up the equipment.

UNDERTAKING A DAY HIKE

Objective: A day hike is an excellent way for scouts to engage with nature while learning navigation, map reading, and team coordination. It helps develop physical endurance and fosters respect for the environment.

- **Plan the Route:** Choose a short, safe hiking trail.
- **Pack Essentials:** Carry water, snacks, a first aid kit, and map/compass.
- **Safety:** Walk at a steady pace, take breaks, and stay together as a group.
- **Leave No Trace:** Make sure to clean up any trash and respect nature.

PARTICIPATING IN A NIGHT GAME

Objective: Night games foster teamwork, enhance problem-solving skills, and allow scouts to develop an awareness of their surroundings in the dark. It also builds trust and confidence in the group.

- **Choose a Safe Game:** Games like hide-and-seek or scavenger hunts are ideal for the dark.
- **Safety First:** Ensure everyone has a flashlight and wears visible clothing.
- **Teamwork:** Scouts work together in teams, communicating and problem-solving.
- **Reflection:** After the game, discuss the experience and lessons learned.

COOKING

BACKWOODSMAN METHOD FOR COOKING

The Backwoodsman Method for cooking is a traditional outdoor cooking technique often used by Scouts, particularly in wilderness settings where simple tools and minimal equipment are available. The method emphasizes cooking over an open fire, using natural materials and minimal preparation.

Steps for the Backwoodsman Method

1. **Gather Materials:** Collect wood for the fire, ensuring it is dry. Gather stones for creating a fire ring and possibly a grill. Collect twigs, branches, and logs for the cooking fire.
2. **Build a Fire:** Set up a safe fire pit, using stones to create a fire ring. Light the fire, ensuring it produces an even, steady heat. The fire can be used directly for cooking or as a heat source to boil water.
3. **Cook Using Simple Equipment:**
    - **Skewers:** Cook food like meat, fish, or vegetables on sticks or skewers directly over the fire.
    - **Pot and Pan Cooking:** If a pot or pan is available, place it over the fire to cook soups, stews, or rice. Ensure you have proper tools to handle hot cookware (like sticks or gloves).

- **Hot Stones:** Sometimes, heated stones can be placed in cooking pots or used directly to cook food. A common method is using flat stones to cook food directly on the surface or in a hole in the ground.

4. **Cooking in the Ground:** Dig a shallow pit and line it with heated stones, then cover with earth. This technique is used for roasting whole animals or large chunks of food, like potatoes.
5. **Cooking with the Fire:** Directly cook food by placing it near the flame or using embers for slow cooking. You can also hang a pot or kettle over the fire on a tripod or a stick arrangement to boil or simmer food.
6. **Safety:** Ensure the fire is carefully controlled and only used in safe areas. Always have a method of extinguishing the fire, such as water or dirt, in case of emergencies.

Uses of the Backwoodsman Method:

- **Survival Skills:** Ideal for Scouts who want to learn wilderness survival skills by cooking with minimal equipment.
- **Outdoor Adventure:** It's great for outdoor camps, especially when traditional cooking tools aren't available.
- **Teamwork:** Scouts can work together to prepare meals, enhancing their teamwork and resourcefulness in the wild.

The Backwoodsman Method allows Scouts to connect with nature while learning practical skills to cook in outdoor settings using natural resources.

SIGNALLING

MORSE SIGNALLING

Morse Signalling is an important method of communication used by Scouts to send messages through the use of dots (short signals) and dashes (long signals). It can be sent using various mediums like sound (via a buzzer), light (using torches), or visual signals (using flags), and is essential for communication when other methods like voice or semaphore are not practical.

Scout must be able to send & receive simple messages of ten words.

Morse Code Chart

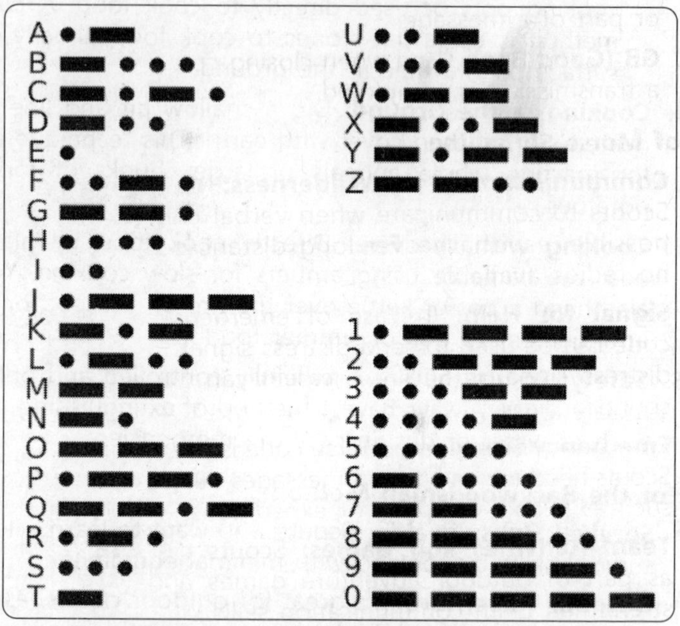

Common Morse Signals and Their Meaning

1. **VE VE VE (Calling up signal):** This is a general signal used to initiate communication. It's like saying "Hello" in Morse Code.
2. **K (Carry On):** Used as a response to VE VE VE, meaning "I'm ready to receive your message."
3. **Q (Wait):** Used as a response to VE VE VE, meaning "I'm not ready to receive your message yet."
4. **T (General Answer):** Used to acknowledge a message or signify a general reply.
5. **AAA (Period or Decimal):** Used to indicate a pause or a decimal point, commonly used when transmitting numerical information.
6. **AR (End of Message):** Signifies that the message has ended and no further communication will follow.
7. **R (Message Received Correctly):** Used to acknowledge that a message has been received properly.

8. **8 dots (Erase):** Used to erase or cancel the previous message or part of a message.
9. **GB (Good Bye):** Used when closing communication or when a transmission is completed.

Uses of Morse Signalling

- **Communication in the Wilderness:** Morse signalling allows Scouts to communicate when verbal communication is not possible, especially over long distances or when there are no radios available.
- **Signal for Help:** In case of emergency situations, Morse code can be used to send distress signals. The most common distress signal is SOS (...), which can be transmitted using sound or light.
- **Emergency Signalling:** Morse code is particularly useful when Scouts need to send urgent messages during outdoor activities, such as hiking, camping, or expeditions.
- **Team Activities and Games:** Scouts can use Morse code as part of outdoor adventure games and as a method to strengthen team communication skills.

PROFICIENCY BADGES

Scouts and Guides must earn proficiency in two specific areas, one from each of the following groups. This ensures that they acquire a diverse set of skills that will benefit them in both personal growth and community service.

S.No.	Group A	S.No.	Group B
1.	Civil Defence	1.	Citizen
2.	Community Worker	2.	Book Binder
3.	Ecologist	3.	Naturalist
4.	Oarsman	4.	Path Finder
5.	Pioneer	5.	Aids Awareness
6.	World Conservation	6.	Healthy Man
7.	Safety Knowledge	7.	Drug Awareness
8.	Self Defence	8.	Boatman
		9.	Computer Awareness

SCOUTING KNOWLEDGE

KNOWLEDGE OF SCOUTING IN INDIA

Scouting in India traces its roots back to the early 20th century. The movement has played a significant role in shaping young people's lives, promoting values such as discipline, patriotism, teamwork, and community service.

1. History:

- Scouting in India began in 1909, with the first Scout camp organized by Sir William H. P. H. MacLean in 1909.
- The movement grew rapidly, with the establishment of several Scout groups across India. The Scout movement in India was officially recognized by the Government of India in 1913.

2. The Bharat Scouts and Guides (BSG):

- The Bharat Scouts and Guides (BSG) is the national Scouting organization in India. It was founded in 1950 by the merger of the Boy Scouts Association and the Girl Guides Association of India.
- It is one of the largest Scout organizations in the world, with millions of members, both male and female, spread across rural and urban areas of India.
- The BSG operates under the guidance of the Ministry of Youth Affairs and Sports, Government of India, and follows the principles of Scouting such as self-reliance, discipline, and community service.

3. Key Programs and Activities:

- BSG organizes various programs for youth, including outdoor activities like camping, hiking, and environmental service projects.
- Scouts and Guides are trained in a range of skills, such as first aid, knot tying, map reading, and leadership.
- The organization also participates in national and international events like Jamborees, where Scouts from around the world come together for activities and cultural exchange.

4. **Development:**
   - The Bharat Scouts and Guides play a significant role in the social and educational development of young people, emphasizing values like social justice, leadership, respect for diversity, and environmental sustainability.

WORLD ORGANISATION OF SCOUT MOVEMENT (WOSM)

The World Organisation of the Scout Movement (WOSM) is the international body that coordinates and supports the Scouting movement globally. It promotes Scouting as a tool for developing young people into responsible, active citizens and leaders.

History

- WOSM was founded in 1920 at the first World Scout Jamboree in London. It was established to bring together national Scout organizations from across the globe to promote the ideals of Scouting.
- WOSM grew from a handful of countries to over 170 countries today, including India, each with its own national Scout organization, such as the Bharat Scouts and Guides.

Mission and Objectives

- The mission of WOSM is to contribute to the education of young people through a value-based, non-political approach to help them achieve their full physical, intellectual, social, and spiritual potential.
- It aims to promote peace, tolerance, solidarity, and understanding among young people from all parts of the world, helping them build a better and more just world.

Structure and Leadership

- WOSM is a non-governmental, non-profit organization governed by its member Scout organizations. It operates through a General Assembly (composed of representatives from member organizations) and is led by a Secretary General and a team based in Geneva, Switzerland.

- The WOSM Board is responsible for overseeing the work of the global organization and coordinating international events, policies, and initiatives.

World Scout Jamboree

- One of the major events organized by WOSM is the World Scout Jamboree, which is held every four years and brings together Scouts from around the world. It is a large gathering that includes cultural exchanges, adventure activities, and educational sessions on global issues.
- The Jamboree provides Scouts with the opportunity to learn about different cultures, forge lasting friendships, and engage in global peace-building efforts.

SAFETY MEASURES

USING ATM CARD AND MOBILE PHONE

ATM Card Safety

- **Protect Your PIN:** Always keep your Personal Identification Number (PIN) private. Do not share it with anyone, even if they claim to be from your bank.
- **Use Secure ATMs:** Choose ATMs in well-lit, secure locations, preferably inside bank branches. Check for any unusual attachments or devices on the ATM that might be used for card skimming.
- **Cover Your PIN:** While entering your PIN at an ATM, always cover the keypad with your hand to prevent anyone from seeing it.
- **Do Not Share Card Details:** Never share your ATM card details, PIN, or one-time passwords (OTPs) over the phone, email, or messages, even if someone claims to be from your bank.
- **Check Account Statements:** Regularly monitor your bank account and ATM transactions to detect any unauthorized activities.

Mobile Phone Safety

- **Lock Your Phone:** Always set up a screen lock (PIN, pattern, fingerprint, or face recognition) to prevent unauthorized access.
- **Avoid Public Wi-Fi for Transactions:** Do not conduct banking or any sensitive transactions over public Wi-Fi, as it could be unsafe. Use mobile data or a secure network instead.
- **Install Trusted Apps Only:** Download apps only from trusted sources like Google Play Store or Apple App Store. Avoid third-party app stores as they could contain malware.
- **Use Mobile Security Software:** Install and regularly update antivirus or anti-malware software on your mobile phone to protect against threats.
- **Be Cautious with Phishing Attacks:** Do not click on suspicious links or open attachments in unsolicited emails or messages, as they could be phishing attempts to steal your information.

FIRE PRECAUTIONS

- **Check Electrical Equipment:** Regularly inspect electrical appliances, wiring, and power sources for damage or wear. Avoid overloading power sockets and switch off electrical appliances when not in use.
- **Proper Storage of Flammable Materials:** Store flammable materials (like fuel, oils, and cleaning agents) in a well-ventilated area away from heat sources.
- **Smoke Detectors:** Install smoke detectors in key areas of your home, especially in the kitchen, near bedrooms, and hallways. Regularly check and replace batteries.
- **Safe Cooking Practices:** Never leave cooking food unattended, especially when using a stove, deep fryer, or grill. Keep flammable materials away from heat sources.
- **Fire Extinguisher Availability:** Keep a fire extinguisher in an accessible location, especially in the kitchen and near any high-risk areas. Learn how to use it properly.

SERVICE

UNDERSTANDING TUBERCULOSIS - SYMPTOMS, TREATMENT, AND PREVENTIVE MEASURES

Tuberculosis (TB) is an infectious disease that mainly affects the lungs but can also affect other parts of the body. It is caused by bacteria that spread through the air when a person with TB coughs, sneezes, or talks. If not treated properly, TB can be dangerous and even fatal.

Symptoms of Tuberculosis

1. **Cough:** A persistent cough lasting more than three weeks, often with blood or sputum.
2. **Chest Pain:** Pain in the chest when breathing or coughing.
3. **Fatigue:** Feeling constantly tired or weak.
4. **Fever and Night Sweats:** A high fever and excessive sweating at night.
5. **Weight Loss:** Unexplained weight loss or loss of appetite.
6. **Shortness of Breath:** Difficulty in breathing, especially in severe cases.
7. **Chills:** Sudden chills or shivering.

Treatment of Tuberculosis

TB is treated with medicines that help kill the bacteria causing the disease. The treatment is usually **long-term, lasting 6 to 9 months.** You will need to take the medicine every day for the full duration to ensure you are fully cured and to prevent the bacteria from becoming resistant to the drugs. It is important to follow the treatment plan strictly and take the medicines even if you start feeling better. If you stop the medication early, the disease might come back, and the bacteria could become harder to treat. Regular follow-ups and tests (such as sputum tests or chest X-rays) are also done to ensure the effectiveness of the treatment and to check for any side effects.

Preventive Measures

1. **Vaccination:** The Bacille Calmette-Guérin (BCG) vaccine can help prevent TB, especially in children.

2. **Good Hygiene:** Covering the mouth and nose when coughing or sneezing to prevent the spread of TB germs.
3. **Proper Ventilation:** Ensuring proper air circulation in living spaces to reduce the concentration of TB bacteria in the air.
4. **Avoid Close Contact:** People with active TB should avoid close contact with others until they are no longer contagious.
5. **Early Diagnosis:** Early detection and treatment of TB are crucial to prevent its spread and complications.
6. **Health Check-ups:** Regular health check-ups and TB screenings for people in high-risk areas (e.g., crowded living conditions, healthcare workers).

KNOWLEDGE ABOUT DIRECTLY OBSERVED TREATMENT

Directly Observed Treatment (DOT) is a method used to make sure that people with TB take their medication correctly and complete their full treatment. This is important because skipping doses or stopping treatment early can lead to the disease coming back or becoming harder to treat.

In DOT, a trained healthcare worker or sometimes a family member, watches the patient take their medicine every day. This ensures that:

- The patient **doesn't forget** to take the medicine.
- The treatment is **completed** fully, reducing the risk of the TB bacteria becoming resistant to the medicine.

Steps in DOT

1. **Watching the Patient:** A healthcare worker makes sure the person takes the TB medicine correctly, usually every day.
2. **Regular Monitoring:** The patient is regularly monitored to check if the treatment is working or if there are any side effects from the medicines.
3. **Support and Encouragement:** The healthcare worker or family member provides emotional support and encouragement to help the patient stay motivated to complete the treatment.

Importance

- **Prevents Drug-Resistant TB:** TB bacteria can become resistant to treatment if the patient doesn't follow the treatment plan. DOT helps prevent this by making sure the patient takes the right medicines on time.
- **Better Recovery:** By ensuring patients take their medicine every day, DOT improves the chances of a full recovery.
- **Prevents Spreading TB:** When treatment is followed properly, the patient is less likely to spread TB to others in the community.

Challenges

- **Access to Healthcare:** In some areas, it might be hard for people to visit the healthcare provider regularly for DOT.
- **Patient Cooperation:** Some patients may forget or may not want to take their medicine every day, making it hard to complete the treatment.
- **Resources:** DOT programs require healthcare workers, medicines, and time, and in some places, these resources might be limited.

How DOT Helps

- **Stops TB from Becoming Hard to Treat:** DOT ensures patients finish their treatment, which helps prevent TB from becoming harder to treat.
- **Reduces the Spread of TB:** By completing the treatment, a person with TB is less likely to infect others in the community.
- **Ensures Better Health:** DOT helps patients recover fully from TB and leads to better overall health outcomes.

A Tritiya Sopan Scout/Guide will work for at least nine months to qualify for Rajya Puraskar Badge.

CHAPTER

6 RAJYA PURASKAR

The Rajya Puraskar, also known as the Governor's Award, is one of the highest honour that a Scout or Guide can achieve at the State level. This prestigious award is bestowed upon Scouts and Guides who are at least 13 years old, have received training from a qualified Scout Master or Guide Captain, and have successfully undergone a State-level assessment conducted by a team of certified examiners.

To be eligible for this award, Scouts and Guides must first earn the requisite qualifying badges. Afterward, they must attend a Rajya Puraskar Testing Camp organised by the State Association, under the supervision of the State Organising Commissioner. During this camp, the knowledge and skills of the Scouts and Guides will be reassessed. The examination for this award is structured to assess both theoretical knowledge and practical skills, reflecting the values and principles that Scouts and Guides uphold. Upon successful completion of this evaluation, the awardees will be presented with the Rajya Puraskar Badge and Certificate.

Requirements:

- Demonstrate proficiency in all tests up to the Tritiya Sopan level.
- Hold the Tritiya Sopan Badge.
- Earn the Ambulance Man Badge.
- Complete an overnight hike of 10 km with a group of Scouts from the same Troop and submit the report to the Scout Master within 10 days.
    - ❑ Alternatively, complete an overnight cycle hike of 30 km with a group of Scouts from the same Troop and submit the report to the Scout Master within 10 days.

OUTDOOR ACTIVITIES

Scouts and Guides are encouraged to select one of the following activities, work on it for six months, and maintain a report to showcase their progress and learning. These projects aim to promote self-reliance, creativity, and teamwork while contributing positively to the environment and society.

At the end of six months, participants must submit a report that can include the following points:

1. **Introduction:** State why the specific project was chosen.
2. **Process:** Detail the steps taken, tools used, and methods followed.
3. **Challenges:** Mention difficulties faced and solutions implemented.
4. **Results:** Share observations, photographs, and benefits gained from the project.
5. **Conclusion:** Reflect on the learning experience and its impact.

KITCHEN GARDEN

A kitchen garden is a small, dedicated area of land or space near the kitchen or home where fruits, vegetables, herbs, and other edible plants are grown. It is meant for personal consumption, promoting fresh and healthy food while reducing dependency on store-bought produce.

Steps to Work on a Kitchen Garden

1. **Choose a Location:** Select a sunny spot in your backyard or any available space with good soil.
2. **Prepare the Soil:** Dig the soil, remove weeds, and enrich it with compost or organic fertilisers.
3. **Select Plants:** Choose seasonal vegetables or herbs like tomatoes, spinach, or coriander.
4. **Planting:** Sow seeds or plant saplings at the appropriate depth and spacing.
5. **Watering and Care:** Water the plants regularly and protect them from pests using natural remedies like neem oil.
6. **Harvest:** After a few weeks or months, harvest the produce and note the yield.

ROOF GARDEN

A roof garden is a garden created on the rooftop of a building, where plants, flowers, or even vegetables are cultivated. It utilises unused rooftop space to add greenery, improve air quality, and regulate building temperatures.

Steps to Work on a Roof Garden

1. **Check Roof Suitability:** Ensure the roof can bear the weight of pots and plants.
2. **Set Up Containers:** Use pots, grow bags, or recycled containers.
3. **Soil and Fertiliser:** Fill containers with a mix of soil and compost.
4. **Planting:** Grow a mix of flowering plants, vegetables, or small fruit trees.
5. **Regular Maintenance:** Water the plants, prune them, and keep an eye out for pests.
6. **Enhance:** Add decorative plants or vertical gardening setups for aesthetics.

HANGING GARDEN

A hanging garden is a decorative garden where plants are grown in containers, pots, or other hanging setups. These gardens are ideal for small spaces, providing greenery and aesthetic appeal without taking up ground space.

Steps to Work on a Hanging Garden

1. **Select Containers:** Use hanging pots, old bottles, or tin cans.
2. **Choose Plants:** Opt for lightweight and low-maintenance plants like ferns, money plants, or herbs.
3. **Set Up:** Use sturdy hooks and ropes to hang the containers at a convenient height.
4. **Soil and Planting:** Use lightweight soil and plant suitable saplings.
5. **Watering:** Ensure proper drainage to avoid water logging.
6. **Enhance the Design:** Add colourful pots or creative arrangements to make it visually appealing.

NATURE COLLECTION

Nature collection involves gathering natural items like leaves, flowers, seeds, stones, feathers, or shells to study, preserve, and display. It fosters a deeper connection with nature and helps in understanding biodiversity.

Steps for Nature Collection

1. **Choose a Theme:** Decide what you want to collect, e.g., leaves of different trees or feathers.
2. **Explore:** Visit parks, forests, or your locality to collect items.
3. **Document:** Note down details like where and when you collected the item.
4. **Preserve:** Use pressing techniques for leaves or boxes for seeds and stones.
5. **Label and Display:** Arrange your collection in a scrapbook or display board with proper labels.
6. **Research and Learn:** Study the items and add interesting facts about them.

MAPPING

PLANE TABLE METHOD

This method involves creating a detailed map using a simple and practical setup, following the principles of triangulation. It is ideal for scouting activities like mapping campsites or patrol areas and teaches fundamental cartographic skills.

Materials Needed

- A sturdy tea chest or box as a table.
- Drawing board and paper.
- Two pins for sighting.
- Pencil and ruler.
- Measuring tape or chain.

STEPS TO CREATE THE MAP

Step 1: Estimate and Scale

- Look around the area. Let's say the campsite is 30 meters wide.
- Decide on a scale for your map. If your paper is 30 cm wide, use a scale of 1 cm = 1 meter.

Step 2: Pick Two Sighting Points

- Choose two points near the centre of the area, such as the corner of your tent (Point "A") and a tree (Point "B").
- Measure the distance between these two points with the tape and note it.

Step 3: Start at Point "A"

- Place your plane table (drawing board) at Point "A".
- Mark Point "A" on the paper using a pin or a dot.
- Place another pin at Point "B", and use the ruler to draw a straight line from Point "A" to Point "B on the paper. This line is your datum line.

Step 4: Plot Features from Point "A"

- Look at features like the gate and another tree from Point "A.
- Align a pin with each feature, using the first pin as a guide.
- Use the ruler to draw lines from Point "A" through these pin positions to represent the direction of each feature.

Step 5: Move to Point "B"

- Now, move the table to Point "B".
- Start by sighting back to Point "A" and aligning it with the datum line you drew earlier.
- Repeat the process of sighting features (tent, gate, tree) from Point "B.
- Draw lines from Point "B" to each feature.

Step 6: Mark Positions on the Map

- The intersection of the lines drawn from Point "A" and Point "B" will give the exact positions of the tent, gate, and tree.

Step 7: Final Touches

- Add labels for each feature (e.g., "Tent," "Gate," "Tree").
- Draw neat symbols for features (like a triangle for a tent or a rectangle for a gate).
- Add a title, scale, and a north arrow to complete the map.

CAMP CRAFT

SINGLE AND DOUBLE FLY TENT

Both Single Fly Tents and Double Fly Tents are commonly used in camping, especially in scouting activities.

- **Single Fly Tent:** A single fly tent consists of one layer of fabric that serves as both the tent walls and the outer protective cover (flysheet). It is lightweight, simple to set up, and ideal for dry, mild weather conditions. However, it offers limited protection against rain, wind, and condensation. It is more portable and cost-effective but lacks the added durability and weather resistance of a double fly tent.
- **Double Fly Tent:** A double fly tent features two layers—an inner tent for sleeping and a separate outer flysheet that provides added protection against the elements. It is designed to offer superior protection from rain, wind, and cold, while also improving ventilation and reducing condensation. Although heavier and more expensive, it is more durable and suitable for longer trips or harsh weather conditions.

Feature	Single Fly Tent	Double Fly Tent
Layers	One (single fabric layer)	Two (inner tent + outer flysheet)
Setup	Quick and simple	Takes more time and effort
Weather Protection	Basic (limited rain/wind protection)	Superior (better rain/wind/cold protection)
Weight & Portability	Lightweight, compact	Heavier, less portable
Comfort	Basic comfort	Better comfort, especially in bad weather
Cost	Less expensive	More expensive
Durability	Less durable	More durable and long-lasting

PATROL PIONEERING PROJECT

Scouts and Guides are required to make a Patrol Pioneering Project which refers to a group activity where a patrol (a small team of scouts or guides) plans, designs, and builds a pioneering structure using ropes, wooden poles, and other available materials. This project aims to develop teamwork, leadership, problem-solving skills, and practical knowledge of knots and lashings.

The following key steps and principles can be taken as reference for a Patrol Pioneering Project:

- **Planning and Design:** The patrol members discuss and decide on the structure to be built, such as a bridge, tower, camp furniture, or a flagpole. They plan how to use the materials efficiently, considering the size and strength needed for the project.
- **Materials Selection:** Scouts and guides choose suitable materials for the project. This typically includes ropes (for lashing), wooden poles (for framing), and any other necessary materials. They must consider the availability of materials and the conditions under which the structure will be used.
- **Building the Structure:** Using basic pioneering techniques such as different types of lashings (square lashing, diagonal lashing, etc.), scouts and guides work together to construct the chosen structure. They must ensure the construction is safe, secure, and durable. The project emphasises the importance of teamwork, precision, and safety.
- **Learning Key Skills:** During the project, scouts and guides learn essential skills such as knot tying (e.g., bowline, clove hitch, etc.), proper use of tools, and teamwork. The ability to follow instructions and take responsibility for different parts of the project is also emphasised.
- **Completion and Evaluation:** Once the structure is completed, the patrol evaluates its strength and functionality. They can test the structure under safe conditions to see if it performs its intended function (e.g., supporting weight, withstanding wind, etc.). Feedback is provided, and improvements or modifications are made if necessary.

- **Reflection and Reporting:** After the project, scouts and guides reflect on the experience, discussing what they learned, the challenges they faced, and how they overcame them. They may also submit a report on their project, which could include photographs, drawings, or explanations of the process.

SCOUTING RESOURCES

KNOWLEDGE ABOUT THE BSG WEBSITE

The Bharat Scouts and Guides (BSG) website, https://www.bsgindia.org/, serves as the official online portal for the Bharat Scouts and Guides, a prominent youth organisation in India. The website provides various resources, updates, and information related to scouting and guiding activities, events, and achievements in India.

Below are some of the main features and information typically available on the BSG website:

1. **About the Organisation:** The website provides detailed information about the history, vision, mission, and objectives of the Bharat Scouts and Guides. It also highlights the principles and values that guide the activities of scouts and guides in India.
2. **Scouting Programs and awards:** It offers details on various scouting programs, training sessions, and events organised for scouts and guides. It also showcases the achievements and contributions of the BSG in the development of young people in India.
3. **Events and News:** The site keeps scouts, guides, and leaders updated with the latest news, upcoming events, camps, and competitions. It provides updates on national and international scouting events.
4. **Publications and Resources:** Educational materials, publications, handbooks, and other resources for scouts and guides are available on the website. This includes useful guides for various scouting activities, safety protocols, and advancement requirements.
5. **Gallery:** The website often features a photo and video gallery showcasing various scouting activities, camps, and events that have taken place across India.

6. **Youth Development:** The website emphasises the role of scouting and guiding in the personal development of youth, helping them grow into responsible citizens with leadership, discipline, and service values.
7. **Contact Information:** The website offers contact details for various BSG offices, including national headquarters, state offices, and local units, for those seeking more information or wishing to reach out to the organisation.

GAINING INFORMATION ABOUT YOUR REGION.

Scouts are required to gain information about their region as it is an important aspect of scouting, helping scouts understand their surroundings and develop awareness about their local area. This activity is valuable for building a sense of community, fostering environmental awareness, and enhancing skills such as navigation, observation, and research.

The following points can be considered to gain information about your region:

- **Learning Geography:** Identify landmarks, terrain, and physical features like rivers and mountains.
- **Studying History and Culture:** Understand local traditions, festivals, and historical events.
- **Exploring Flora and Fauna:** Recognise native plants, animals, and ecosystems.
- **Engaging with the Community:** Interact with local people and participate in community events.
- **Using Maps and Navigation:** Learn map reading and navigation tools like compass and GPS.
- **Understanding the Economy:** Know about local industries, resources, and environmental issues.

This knowledge will build awareness, promote community involvement, and will help scouts to connect with their surroundings.

A Rajya Puraskar Scout/Guide shall work for at least twelve months to appear for Rashtrapati Scout/Guide Award.

CHAPTER 7

RASHTRAPATI SCOUT AWARD

The Rashtrapati Scout Award is one of the most prestigious recognitions in the Bharat Scouts and Guides. It honours a Scout's outstanding skills, leadership, and commitment to community service and personal development.

REQUIREMENTS

To earn this award, a Scout must fulfil the following criteria:

- **State Award Requirement:** The Scout must hold the Rajya Puraskar and consistently maintain the high standards associated with it.
- **Camping Requirements:**
    - ❑ **Overnight Camping:** The Scout must camp with their Company or Patrol for three consecutive nights in the open (large gatherings such as Jamborees or Rallies do not count).
    - ❑ **Shelter Construction:** The Scout should demonstrate the ability to improvise a shelter, hut, or machan using natural materials available on-site, providing adequate space for two persons to sleep.
- **Badge Requirements:**
    - ❑ The Scout must hold the Disaster Management Badge.
    - ❑ Additionally, the Scout must re-pass the Ambulance Badge, ensuring proficiency in emergency response and first aid.

These requirements are designed to promote a balanced development of practical outdoor skills, emergency preparedness, leadership, and community service. Earning the Rashtrapati Scout Award is a mark of excellence that reflects a Scout's readiness to take on greater respnosibilities and contribute positively to society.

PROFICIENCY BADGES

The Scout should qualify for any two of the following Proficiency Badges that have not been earned previously:

- Aids Awareness
- Beautician
- Sea Fisherwoman
- World Conservation
- Farmer
- Solar Energy Awareness
- Self Defence
- Handywoman
- Pathfinder
- Hiker
- Interpreter
- Free Being Me
- Event Manager

COMMUNITY DEVELOPMENT PROJECT

Scouts and guides are required to participate in a community development project for six months with a commitment of at least two hours a week which can have a significant positive impact.

PROMOTE GENDER EQUALITY AND WOMEN EMPOWERMENT

Gender Equality means that individuals, regardless of their gender, have equal rights, opportunities, and treatment in all areas of life such as education, employment, and political participation. It aims to eliminate discrimination based on gender.

Women Empowerment refers to the process of enhancing women's ability to make choices, access resources, and control their own lives. This includes promoting women's participation in decision-making, ensuring equal rights, and addressing gender-based violence.

Promoting Gender Equality and Empowering Women involves raising awareness about equal rights and opportunities for women, advocating for their participation in decision-making, and eliminating gender-based violence. The aim is to ensure that women have access to education, employment, healthcare, and leadership roles, fostering equality in society.

Activities: Organise awareness campaigns on gender equality, conduct workshops on women's rights, encourage leadership roles for women in community activities, and create safe spaces for women to discuss their issues.

REDUCING CHILD MORTALITY

Child mortality refers to the death of children under the age of five. This often results from preventable causes such as poor nutrition, lack of proper healthcare, infections, unsafe water, and malnutrition. Reducing child mortality is a major global health goal.

Activities: Promote health awareness programs about immunisation, proper nutrition, and sanitation. Help in organising vaccination drives, and teach parents about the importance of regular health checkups for children.

IMPROVING MATERNAL HEALTH

Maternal health refers to the health of women during pregnancy, childbirth, and the postpartum period. It focuses on ensuring that women have access to the necessary healthcare and resources to prevent complications, promote healthy pregnancies, and reduce the risk of maternal death or illness during and after childbirth.

Activities: Educate the community about prenatal care, safe deliveries, post-natal care, and the importance of nutrition during pregnancy. Support local health clinics by volunteering in organising maternal health checkups.

COMBATING HIV/AIDS, MALARIA, AND OTHER DISEASES

HIV (Human Immunodeficiency Virus) is a virus that attacks the immune system, making the body vulnerable to infections. AIDS (Acquired Immunodeficiency Syndrome) is the final stage of HIV infection when the immune system is severely weakened.

Malaria is a life-threatening disease caused by parasites that are transmitted to humans through the bites of infected mosquitoes. It can be prevented and treated with medication.

Activities: Educate people on preventive measures for diseases like HIV/AIDS and malaria. Distribute educational materials, support awareness campaigns, and help in community-level health services like mosquito net distribution and HIV testing.

ENSURING ENVIRONMENTAL SUSTAINABILITY

Environmental sustainability is the practice of using natural resources in a way that does not deplete or harm the environment, ensuring that future generations can enjoy the same or better quality of life. It includes conserving water, reducing pollution, protecting biodiversity, using renewable energy, and promoting sustainable agriculture and waste management. The goal is to preserve the planet's health while supporting economic growth and human well-being. Key actions include waste management, water conservation, tree planting, promoting renewable energy, and educating communities on how to use resources in ways that do not deplete or damage the environment.

Activities: Take part in environmental conservation activities like tree planting, waste management drives, and educating communities on sustainable farming practices and water conservation.

INFORMATION ABOUT

KANDERSTEG ADVENTURE CENTRE OF WOSM IN SWITZERLAND

Kandersteg International Scout Centre (KISC), located in Kandersteg, Switzerland, is the only officially recognised World Scout Centre by the World Organisation of the Scout Movement (WOSM). The centre is nestled in the Swiss Alps and offers a unique setting for Scouts and non-Scouts to experience outdoor activities and connect with nature.

- **Founded:** February 12, 1923
  - **Founders:** Robert Baden-Powell (the founder of the Scouting Movement) and Walther von Bonstetten (a Swiss Scout leader).
  - **Mission:** KISC was inspired by Baden-Powell's vision of a Permanent Mini Jamboree, where Scouts from around the world could gather and work towards creating a better world through unity, peace, and sustainability.
  - **Location:** Kandersteg, Switzerland, located in the heart of the Swiss Alps.
  - **Facilities:** The centre spans 17 hectares and offers a variety of accommodation options, including lodges, chalets, and campsites. It is an ideal location for outdoor activities such

as hiking, mountaineering, swimming in alpine lakes, and stargazing.

- **Open Year-Round:** KISC is open throughout the year to Scouts and, for most of the year, also to non-Scouts.

Kandersteg International Scout Centre (KISC) offers a wide range of outdoor activities that focus on environmental sustainability and the core Scouting values of adventure, teamwork, and community. Scouts visiting KISC can engage in climbing and mountaineering in the stunning Alps, enjoy swimming in the crystal-clear alpine lakes, and participate in cultural exchanges with Scouts from around the world. The centre promotes sustainability, peace, and global friendship, reflecting the mission of the Scout Movement. Since its establishment, KISC has played a vital role in fostering international cooperation and unity, providing a unique space for Scouts to connect, collaborate, and embrace the principles of Scouting in an inspiring natural environment. More than just a campsite, KISC embodies the Scout Movement's dedication to bringing people together to create a better, more harmonious world.

ASIA PACIFIC SCOUT REGION

The Asia-Pacific Region (APR) of the World Organisation of the Scout Movement (WOSM) is a vital part of the global Scout Movement, covering a vast and diverse geographical area. This region includes about 30 National Scout Organisations (NSOs), spread across East Asia, Southeast Asia, South Asia, and the Pacific Islands. The region is known for its diversity and dynamic activities that promote Scouting's values of friendship, leadership, sustainability, and peace. The APR encourages cross-cultural understanding through events, exchanges, and community service projects, and plays an active role in achieving global goals such as the United Nations Sustainable Development Goals (SDGs).

The Asia-Pacific Region also focuses on collaboration and innovation. One notable project is its partnership with the Open Mapping Hub-Asia Pacific, which enhances disaster preparedness and response through updated map data, ensuring Scouts are equipped to handle humanitarian challenges.

PHOTO GALLERY

Lady Baden Powell with Mrs. Lakshmi Mazumdar at the proposed site of National Headquarter (1960)

President Eisenhower of USA accompanied by Prime Minister Jawahar Lal Nehru being presented a Scarf by a Scout (1959)

Dr. Rajendra Prasad, President of India, being greeted by Chief Commissioner of Common Wealth at New Delhi (1959)

Shri K.N. Katju, Governor of Madhya Pradesh at National Training Centre, Pachmarhi (1956)

Dr. Rajendra Prasad, President of India, with delegates at meeting of Chief Commissioners (Guides), Asian Area meeting held in New Delhi (1956)

Dr. Rajendra Prasad, President of India, addressing Scouters and Guiders during a conference held at New Delhi-Dr. H.N. Kunzru, National Commissioner is seated to his left (1952)

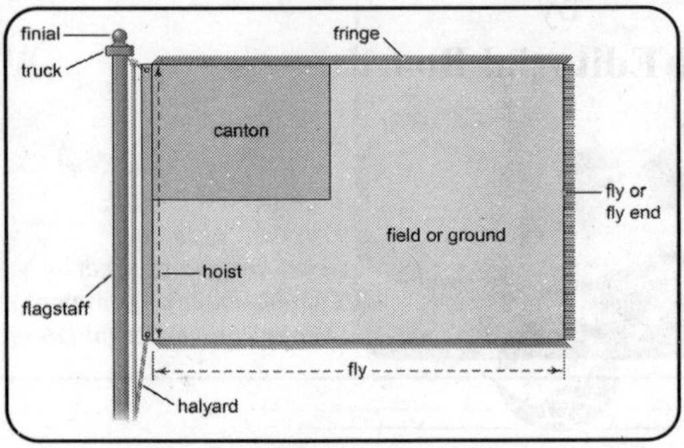

The Parts of a Flag